ADVANCE PRAISE FOR *THE SOUL OF PURPOSE*

"Jaya Jaya Myra does a wonderful job teaching people the connections between good health and mind-body wellbeing. The WELL Method is a great tool for cultivating a positive and grateful mindset about life that can help people heal and regain balance. It's a must-read book on mind, body, and soul wellbeing."
— DR. JOSH AXE, Founder of Ancient Nutrition

"*The Soul of Purpose* is the right book at the right time and will help so many. The WELL Method is a framework to structure the three components that make you: mind, body, and soul. Wherever you are at, this book is the open door to regaining harmony and balance. I will recommend it to my patients."
— DR. JOEL KAHN M.D., Author of *The Whole Heart Solution*

"Jaya Jaya Myra does a phenomenal job explaining the mind-body connection and how to make practical changes in day-to-day life that have a major impact on health and wellness, including finding your purpose. *The Soul of Purpose* is equally inspiring and educational, and a must-read for anyone who wants to live a holistic, healthy life."
— DR. DAVID FRIEDMAN, Author of *Food Sanity: How to Eat in a World of Fads and Fiction*

"Jaya Jaya Myra shows the profound connection between purpose and health and how potent cultivating holistic wellbeing can be. *The Soul of Purpose* is an inspiring and important book, especially during a pandemic, for practical guidance on mind, body, and soul wellbeing."
— PAUL SCHULICK, Founder of New Chapter and For The Biome

"Creating good health and mental wellness is a unique process for every individual, and Jaya Jaya Myra reveals a crucial—frequently overlooked—piece of the puzzle: knowing your purpose. She explains why living your purpose is vital for good health, and shows the reader how to create inner prosperity no matter what's happening in life. An empowering and inspiring journey!"

— CATE MONTANA, MA, Author of *The E Word: Ego, Enlightenment & Other Essentials*

"Jaya Jaya Myra has written a phenomenal book on the connections of purpose, spirituality, and health! *The Soul of Purpose* takes you on a soul-inspiring journey to be the best possible version of yourself, while improving your health and wellbeing, mind, body, and soul. Jaya Jaya Myra has created a must-read book on holistic wellness."

— AMY LEIGH MERCREE, Author of *100 Days to Calm: A Journal for Finding Everyday Tranquility*, *A Little Bit of Goddess*, and *The Mood Book: Crystals, Oils, and Rituals to Elevate Your Spirit*

"Wish that you had the power to get yourself better from fibromyalgia? You do! You won't get it from your physician. But you will get it by learning to follow your own intuition, noticing what feels good to you and what works best for your body. Along with a healthy dose of common sense. Especially important? Knowing that your mind and mindset can be both a powerful healer or a slayer. The choice is up to you. Need a guide? Jaya Jaya Myra is here to help!"

— DR. JACOB TEITELBAUM, Author of *From Fatigued to Fantastic!*

THE SOUL OF PURPOSE

A STEP-BY-STEP APPROACH TO CREATE A PURPOSE-DRIVEN, HEALTHY LIFE

JAYA JAYA MYRA

Post Hill
PRESS

A POST HILL PRESS BOOK
ISBN: 978-1-64293-513-4
ISBN (eBook): 978-1-64293-514-1

The Soul of Purpose:
A Step-By-Step Approach to Create a Purpose-Driven, Healthy Life
© 2021 by Jaya Jaya Myra
All Rights Reserved

Interior charts and graphics by Hayden Brown

Post Hill Press
New York • Nashville
posthillpress.com

Published in the United States of America

DEDICATION

I'd like to dedicate this book to my daughters, Gwenyth and Rhiannon, because you represent the future, and I want you to have everything you need to succeed and thrive in life. This book is your roadmap to your hearts' desires and more. I'd also like to dedicate this book to my dear friend and number one supporter in all ways, Collin. Without you, all of the time, effort, and dedication I've put into this book would not be possible.

TABLE OF CONTENTS

Foreword ix
Introduction xiii

PART I

THE SOUL OF PURPOSE &
THE FOUNDATIONS OF WELL-BEING

Chapter 1: Be Uniquely & Unequivocally You 3

Chapter 2: Inner Prosperity & The Power of Faith 22

Chapter 3: The WELL Method 38

Chapter 4: Identify Your Purpose & Create Your Purpose Plan . . . 55

PART II
THE PATH FROM PURPOSE TO WELLNESS

Chapter 5: Just Breathe 73

Chapter 6: What's Going on in Your Head? 82

Chapter 7: Work with Your Unique Energy Type 95

Chapter 8: Face Your Fears of Change 106

Chapter 9: Food for Mood & Well-being 115

Chapter 10: Let's Shake It! (The Power of Exercise) 130

Chapter 11: Speak No Evil (The Power of Words) 140

Chapter 12: Create Your Sacred Space 151

PART III
THE SETBACKS, SOLUTIONS & VICTORIES

Chapter 13: The Setbacks & Their Solutions 165

Chapter 14: The Victories: Living a Purpose-Driven,
Healthy Life. 175

Chapter 15: Keep Moving Forward (or Conclusion) 182

Acknowledgments. 188
About the Author 189

FOREWORD

In 430 BC, Hippocrates, the "Father of Medicine," said, "Let food be thy medicine and medicine be thy food." Fast-forward to today, and science has proven his statement to be correct! What we eat plays a crucial role in combating conditions like depression, obesity, arthritis, heart disease, type 2 diabetes, and even cancer. But what Hippocrates didn't know 2,450 years ago is how much stress people would be enduring in today's modern world. According to the American Medical Association, 80 percent of all physician office visits are for stress-related ailments. Chronic psychological stress wreaks havoc on the mind and body by causing an inflammatory response. This can promote the development and progression of disease. If Hippocrates were alive today, I believe he would change his famous statement to, "Let stress management be thy medicine."

Stress is the antagonist of a healthy mindset. It can also affect your sleep and activate the production of the hunger hormone called ghrelin, which makes you want to eat! Unfortunately, it's not broccoli or carrot sticks you crave during times of stress-induced sleeplessness, but unhealthy comfort foods. Chronic stress also causes elevated cortisol, the "stress hormone," and a reduction of serotonin, which regulates mood, happiness, and anxiety. Low serotonin levels have been linked to causing depression and a lack of motivation. This stressed-induced hormonal rollercoaster affects everything from our appetite, weight, energy, mood, and sex drive.

The secret to attaining a healthy mind, body, and spirit is to focus on the true meaning of the word *diet*. Diet comes from the Greek word *diaita*, which means "way of living." This includes managing stress, creating a proper mindset, exercising, getting restorative sleep, and developing healthy eating habits. I was thrilled to see all these pillars of good health in Myra's book *The Soul of Purpose*. She offers the complete blueprints everyone needs to reach their optimal health on a physical, mental, and spiritual level.

We all strive to be happier and healthier; however, the daily tension between yesterday's promise of a new tomorrow and the reality of today creates a constant struggle. Myra makes sense out of it all by addressing our lack of physical and emotional ease (*dis-ease*) and then brings all the pieces together through a unique synergistic harmony. Her easy-to-follow blueprints offer a pathway to achieving a total body restoration. Myra discovered these tools for success while battling her own debilitating physical condition that was being fueled by emotional distress. This robbed her of all sense of self-worth and created something she refers to as an "inner poverty" complex. We've all been there to some extent—some of us more than others—not living up to our full potential due to self-sabotaging actions that strip us of our true self-worth. Through a system Myra created called The WELL Method, she was able to successfully recover and regain her inner prosperity. She is now living a life of purpose.

Life is a marathon, not a sprint. Our time on earth is long and arduous and it's important that we pace ourselves. This book shares how *small changes* and consistent habits can add up to *huge differences*. This keeps us from running out of steam before we reach the finish line. Myra does a magnificent job of guiding us to a balanced and healthy life through small, easy-to-follow steps. But there are also times when taking no steps and just *being still* is necessary. Myra teaches how we can use meditation as a way of changing the function of our brain to support self-control. Her "small steps to attaining giant strides" approach gives each of us the ability to harness the power within and reach our desired goals.

Wherever you are in this journey called life, if you've found yourself stuck and in need of overcoming barriers, *The Soul of Purpose* is the book you've been waiting for.

— Dr. David Friedman, Syndicated TV and Radio Health Expert, International award-winning, #1 bestselling author of *Food Sanity*

INTRODUCTION

Overview

What precisely does it mean to live your purpose, and how is this connected to well-being? What does it mean to be in good health mentally, emotionally, spiritually, and physically, and how can you achieve this? Why is well-being considered by millennials and Gen Z to be "the new black," replacing luxury goods as their status symbol of choice? Why is nearly 90 percent of all modern disease attributed to lifestyle choices? And perhaps most importantly, what do you do for your health and well-being when your doctor doesn't even know how to treat you effectively? I'll address all of this and more in this book.

My personal journey to a purposeful life started out as a difficult one because I didn't know what to do or where to start. When I was diagnosed with fibromyalgia (and it was debilitating, to the point that I lost everything in my life), the Western medical approach to treating chronic illness failed me completely. Not only did it fail, it made me feel worse and put me in more physical pain. The side effects of prescribed treatments were worse than the disease I was suffering from. I felt emotionally bankrupt and shackled to a condition no one really knew how to deal with. And how on earth was I supposed to find or fulfill my purpose when I was so physically ill that it hurt to even move?

I knew I had to do something different and find a way to get well because sickness was not an option. Failing at my life's purpose was not an option. I grew up believing that God never gives you something you can't handle, so if this was given to me, there was a purpose in it and reason for it…and that purpose was not meant to hinder me but to help me succeed. I had zero doubt in this—that moment of complete faith that there was a way to heal was the start of my journey.

While on my journey, I came to realize that purpose itself has a soul, and that purpose itself is foundational to everything in life including success, wealth, health, and overall well-being in ways I could have never imagined. This intangible force is responsible for everything that makes you "you" and even plays a major role in your connection with God. It's the fabric that holds this entire creation together and can be utilized in so many different ways to improve any aspect of life. Getting a glimpse into the soul of purpose was the real beginning of finding and fulfilling my life's purpose, as I'd come to realize. You'll learn how foundational purpose is to your life as well.

Background—Why I Developed The WELL Method

First, let me tell you a bit about myself and what brought me to this point in my life. I'm a writer, speaker, and trainer specializing in what I call "wellness lifestyle." My education was in the sciences: specifically, molecular biology. I worked for many years as a research scientist, both in academia and big pharma. I've had a lifelong dream of helping people be well, because I've always known there is a connection to how well you are and what you are able to accomplish. I grew up in a challenging family environment so my hopes and dreams from a very young age were focused on the things I didn't have in my life.

When I was about eight years old, my mom stopped working and went on disability. She had a ruptured disc in her spine and a pinched nerve which prevented her from properly doing her job—or any work for that matter. As if that weren't difficult enough, her health problems continued to get worse year by year. One ruptured disc and pinched nerve turned into several. She suffered from near-constant chronic pain that was uncontrollable even by the strictest and most highly regulated pain medicine available.

Emotionally, she was a wreck. Her husband (my stepfather) was verbally abusive and not supportive at all. My mother used alcohol as a way to cope with it all. Not that alcohol ever does anything productive, but it did make her black out for long periods of time and not know what was going on with herself or with me. The constant awareness of how unwell she was and how her life was spiraling downwards and out of control led to my fierce desire to be able to make people well, not just physically, but mentally and emotionally too. I dreamed big (always have and always will). I wanted to find a way to heal diseases as devastating as cancer or AIDS. Since my mother was constantly unwell, my desire to heal others grew stronger and stronger.

Unfortunately, my mother got progressively worse until her pain finally killed her. She died of a prescription drug overdose when I was just nineteen years old. For eleven years, I watched her condition worsen until it was too much for her to deal with. Her death was deemed accidental, and I have no doubt it was. She always complained about how she'd have to take double or triple the dose of pain medicine to feel any sort of relief. Despite warnings from her doctors about the dangers of overdose, and them directly telling her that she would likely die if she did not follow the proper dosage, she continued to take far too much.

She died alone, with no one to help her. Her "husband" didn't even realize something was wrong until he found her body twelve hours after she was believed to have died. May she rest in peace.

Fortunately for me, I was in good health, and I was optimistic about life. Or so I thought. In 2007, I began having severe headaches, aches and pains, and horrible brain fog. Day-to-day tasks became challenging, and it was difficult to function like a normal person. I was diagnosed with fibromyalgia, and my doctor was ready to put me on full disability. I lost my job, my home, my marriage, and had to declare bankruptcy. My entire life became unrecognizable in a very short period of time.

Having seen firsthand what my mom went through and how it destroyed her life, I wasn't willing to let the same thing happen to me. Even though I didn't know where to start or if I was making the right decisions, I found a way to turn my life around and heal myself naturally, but it was not in any way, shape, or form what I expected the journey would be like. The reality of my situation turned out to be more beautiful than I could possibly imagine. Since I had no idea where to begin my journey towards health, I started with my journey towards purpose. It wasn't until well into this process that I discovered both were part of the same journey and that purpose was foundational to it all. I learned some powerful secrets about success, mental and emotional health, purpose, and overall well-being—all of which I'll share with you. The profound connection between purpose and health can no longer be overlooked.

How This Book is Structured and What You'll Get Out of It

There are many books that talk about purpose, meditation, mind-body-spirit balance, and different approaches to well-being, but what I've found lacking in all of them is a concrete, easy to understand path of what to do and what to expect during the process. Since we are all different, how do you find what will work for you since no one-size-fits-all approach works for everyone? What's the secret to cracking the code? Why is finding and living your purpose so important? What is the journey really like when you're changing your life, inwardly and outwardly, and how is it definitively tied to living your purpose?

In this book, I'll show you exactly how I made sense of it all, identified my purpose, and healed my life naturally, and each step I took to get to where I am now. This book is structured so that each chapter focuses on a new concept and approach, in the order I used each concept in my journey towards purpose and better health. You'll hear from me and other well-known experts about the concepts being discussed. You'll learn exactly how purpose is foundational to wellness, how it's connected to spirituality, and how to use both purpose and spirituality to cultivate a positive, optimistic mindset about life. Lastly, you'll learn how to discover your life's purpose and create a personalized plan to achieve health, wellness, and a purpose-driven life.

Here's what you'll get out of this book:

- Learn why the soul of purpose is foundational to health, wealth, and meaning in life.
- A step-by-step, personalized approach to finding your purpose, health, and wellness based on my own journey and the experiences of other experts.

- You'll learn The WELL Method and how to apply it in your day-to-day life for fulfilled living.
- I'll share the profound connection between spirituality, purpose, and your unique body type that will deepen your faith and inspire you to succeed.
- I'll share the challenges I faced along the way, the things that caused setbacks, and the solutions I found to help me move forward.
- You'll learn the top warning signs that signal you're about to have a setback and how to either avoid one or deal with it when it happens.
- You'll also learn how to get out of "self-destruct mode" and get back on track when you feel like a failure.

Now that you know what to expect, let's begin!

PART I

THE SOUL OF PURPOSE & THE FOUNDATIONS OF WELL-BEING

The 10 Commandments of Wellness

1. To your own self, be true—your health depends on it.

2. Mind, body, and soul are three parts of the same whole—treat them as such.

3. Your soul's purpose determines your physical body's composition, shape, and structure—treat your body like a temple of greatness.

4. You are different from other people—let those differences unite you, not divide you.

5. Consistency is key for building a strong and stable foundation—pick your daily habits wisely.

6. Mindfulness is more than meditation—learn to control your thoughts, moods, and perceptions.

7. Spirituality is how you unite the divided pieces of yourself—let it enable your highest potential.

8. Inner prosperity is the link between possibility and reality—cultivate it daily.

9. When love is sacrificed, so is your capacity for wellness—make wise, heart-centered life decisions.

10. Dreams and goals are your fuel and currency in life—never stop pursuing your dreams.

CHAPTER 1

BE UNIQUELY & UNEQUIVOCALLY YOU

What does it mean to be uniquely, unequivocally you, and how is this related to living your purpose or being in good health? That's a very good question and one you'll probably never look at in quite the same way again. For me, there is so much power in this statement. It's a reflection of the greatness every human being is endowed with from birth. It's our cumulative strengths, talents, and gifts; our weaknesses; and the knowledge that everything we are as individuals is perfect perfection. You are never given anything in life you can't handle, which means for every perceived weakness you have, you've already been given a gift to combat it and minimize the effects of that weakness in your life. Everything that you are is meant to serve your highest calling and life's purpose. While this might sound like a motivational speech meant to uplift you and make you feel better about life, it's so much more. It's actually the nuts and bolts behind how you were made and why: there is a definitive connection between your soul and your life's purpose, and your unique purpose for living shapes your entire physical constitution and personality. Yes, you read that right. Your soul's purpose determines your physical body's shape and structure, your appearance, your health, and the exact talents and gifts you were born with.

Long before you were ever born, God had a plan for you. And since you are a part of God, that means you had a plan for your life. This plan, this grand purpose for your soul to be born in a physical body, is what determines everything about you. Everything that you are is unique to you so that you can best live your purpose and be a light in this world. We are each like a beautiful tapestry, unique in our own ways and each with our own identity. Your uniqueness is a perfect match for you to do what you were born to do.

You're probably wondering why you haven't heard about this before; well, at least the part about how purpose shapes your body type and structure. It comes down to the lens of perception you see something through and also whether or not you're accumulating information or gaining wisdom from it. I'm sure you've heard the saying, "Truth has three versions: my version, your version, and the actual truth." I've found that while Eastern traditions are vastly more expansive in their perspective and knowledge base, even people who study these traditions will still tend to see and understand life through a single lens of perception. For example, if you learn about Ayurveda or traditional Chinese medicine, you'll be learning about health and be taught that mental and emotional well-being plays a role, as does your unique constitution. If you learn about spirituality, you'll be told to find and live your purpose and that well-being is a part of that. Unless you've delved deeply into more than one discipline (and often times even if you do) and you've really grasped it through the information taught and your direct experience (this is wisdom), it's common to not see the interconnecting threads between different perspectives or disciplines. If you do see them, you might take them for granted and not realize how profound the relationship is unless you have a tangible reason to explore it. And why is this? Because those connecting threads are not the focus of either discipline, so our human mind wrongly devalues them. The connection of purpose to health, life, and body type is in those interconnecting threads of spirituality and health that most people never see.

It's in this in-between space where the truly profound lives. It's here where humanity continues to grow and expand its understanding and unity of all things. The interconnecting threads are links in a chain that have always been there; we just haven't noticed them before. I was educated as a scientist. My job was to look for new things, analyze situations and data, and look for new connections. Even before then, when I was growing up and learning about the world, I was taught to try and understand life from multiple points of view so as to show true compassion to people. Those combined experiences made me the type of person who looks for how things are related, and why. To dig in deeply and uncover hidden truths. This is one of my gifts in life and one that I use to help many people. When I found the connecting threads between purpose and health, I became incredibly excited and dug in to learn more. I strongly believe that understanding health from a perspective of purpose and each person's uniqueness is crucial if we are going to continue to grow as humans.

While this is not actively taught in healing systems like Ayurveda or traditional Chinese medicine because it is more the spiritual side of health and well-being, you'll still need to know a bit about the foundations of these systems to understand how the forces of nature shape your body and your personality. Nothing about you is random. You are a masterpiece and an inspiration!

The Five Elemental Types

Both Ayurveda and traditional Chinese medicine (TCM) use a five-element approach to understanding life, health, and all of existence. Each system has a slightly different set of elements, but the overarching principles are vastly similar. Each of the five elements represents a unique force of nature, and, as such, each element has its own unique attributes, strengths, and weaknesses associated with it. For nature to exist in perfect harmony, we need a combination of each of these elemental forces. They will never be in equal balance—nor should they be—because the unique combination of elements is what makes each person unique in their personality and body type. Here's an example: Fire and rain can't both exist together in equal proportions. If you have water, it can put out fire, but fire can also boil water turning it into vapor and air. Each of the elements and their unique combinations have a valuable purpose and function for sustaining life.

Figure 1-1: the elemental components of Ayurveda & TCM.

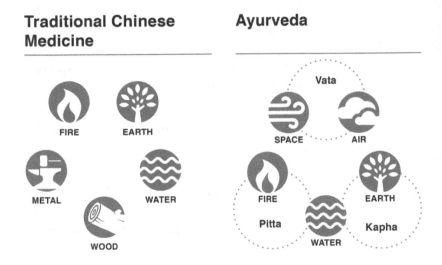

The body is a microcosm of the universe, and the body contains each of the five elemental forces within it—not all in equal amounts, but each in the proportions that they need to be for you to understand and fulfill your purpose for living. Remember, your soul's purpose for living is what determines your unique elemental composition. Each person has a different and unique combination of the five elements, and this is how personality, innate talents, strengths, weaknesses, and body structure are shaped. You are likely to have anywhere from one to three predominant elements in your constitution which will heavily influence your body structure and personality type. Since your elemental type is created from your purpose, understanding your elemental composition can help you identify your purpose for living and provide a roadmap for what's necessary for you to maintain a healthy mind, body, and soul. There are two major pieces of the puzzle to identifying your purpose for living, and elemental composition helps you understand the first piece. We will dive into both as we create your personal plan for healthy, purpose-filled living.

Ayurveda and TCM outline the health and elemental composition connection quite well (that's the point of these disciplines), so I'll focus on how our purpose relates to the expression of elemental attributes in your life. Since you contain all of the elements inside of you, you can leverage any of them as you need, even if it's not your predominant type. Let's look at how the elements shape your personality. If you live your life well and keep things in harmony, you're not apt to see as many negative attributes. If you see these things in your life, you can be assured that you need to cultivate better mind-body-soul harmony. The thing with any attribute is that it's a double-edged sword—nothing is fixed. If you live your life well, an elemental trait will manifest its positive attributes. If you don't live your life well and in relation to your unique temperament, the negative attributes are more likely to manifest.

Figure 1-2: the elements & their psychological & emotional attributes.

Element	Positive Attributes	Negative Attributes
Space/Ether	Subtle awareness and intuition, neutral to praise or criticism, honest, clear communication style, likes to communicate, good design aesthetic, good with shapes, understands personal space.	Dishonest, disregard for rules or authority, lacks respect for others, lives comfortably in one's own world.
Air	Intuitive, open to possibility, sees the big picture, visionary, other-worldly, creative.	Flakey, ungrounded, non-committal, lacks focus and follow through, disconnected from reality.
Fire	Willpower, focus, clarity, confidence, goal-oriented, authoritative, determination, positive attitude.	Domineering, bossy, arrogant, power-hungry, angry, aggressive, abusive, sharp tongue, scattered thoughts, short fuse.
Water	Nurturing, caring, family-oriented, high level of emotional intelligence, good listener, flowing and not rigid, healing ability, always changing.	Overly emotional, easily swayed by others, lacks self-worth, lack of healthy boundaries, gloomy, negative attitude, personality changes depending on who's around.
Earth	Strategic, can see the big picture and the details, grounded and emotionally stable, likes routine, methodical, likes cleanliness, organized.	Laziness, excess sleep, inertia, rigid, fixed beliefs, lack of discipline, packrat, life is full of clutter, very difficult to break old habits or try new things.

As you can see, the elements are a spectrum of different attributes that go from least dense and intangible all the way down to extremely heavy and tangible. Space is the least dense of the elements, and they gradually attain more substance as they progress towards the earth element. People with earth and water as primary elemental types will tend to have larger body structures than people of fire or air body types (think: are you willowy in build or curvy? It's due to your primary elemental type). Note, this does not mean fat, although gaining weight is easier for people with earth or water as their primary elements than it is for people who have fire, air, or space elements as their primary types. If air is a person's primary elemental type, they will likely never be curvy in build, just like someone with a primary earth or eater elemental type will never be considered willowy or gaunt in build.

This provides some very valuable information about how to take care of the body and the types of foods that will make you feel the healthiest and most fulfilled. Foods also have elemental properties to them. Everything in existence has an elemental profile because the five elements are building blocks for everything in the universe. Earthy people in good health tend to eat less earthy foods, and the same is true for other elements as well. If an air-based person ate only light, airy foods like salad, they would never have the stamina to be creative or healthy. If an earthy person ate pasta all the time, they'd end up being sluggish, lethargic, and overweight. Eating in relation to your body type is a key to fighting disease, staying healthy, and optimizing your innate gifts. We will talk about this more later in the book.

When it comes to personality, you can see the progression from formless to tangible as you move from the space element down to the earth element. Space and air elements lend to visionary ideas and creativity which, in and of themselves, lack form, whereas fire, water, and earth lend the substance necessary to give ideas shape and form that make them a reality. While earthy people will tend to have a bulkier or curvier physique, they also tend to have more stamina and are the ones to drive projects to completion, orchestrating the details and following through. In terms of personality, the denser elements are the ones that lead to success in materialistic affairs; after all, it takes a lot of work, stamina, and endurance to turn an idea into a reality.

The fire element sits right in the middle of air and water, and it has the amazing powers to either create or destroy, depending on your point of view and how you use it. Fire is what fuels your drive for success, creates focus, willpower, and the burning, longing desire to succeed. It also has the power to destroy anything that stands in the way of whatever your core desire is. Because of this, the fire element is your wildcard and something to cultivate and learn to use well, even if it's not your primary elemental type. In order for something new to be created, you first have to clear the path by learning to take the energy from one thing and use it to fuel what's being created. Fire gets its fuel from burning other things, turning them to ash and consuming anything that goes into it. If you put a log into a fire, that log will give the fire the energy it needs to burn, then the log will be turned to nothing but ash and charcoal. The log no longer exists. In the body, our digestive process is due to the fire element. We eat food, it gets digested and turned into the nutrients we need to fuel our body and mind. And the cycle continues. In terms of personality, the energy and burning desire that the fire element gives us is the fuel necessary to turn an idea into a reality.

Let's take a moment to look at two different people with two very different primary elemental types and how this shapes their lives. Here's how this might look in a multi-faceted person. Let's use Mary as an example. Mary has an elemental composition with predominance in earth and fire elements. In terms of personality, Mary is very detail-oriented, organized, and methodical. She's a stickler for details (much to the chagrin of Jack, whom we'll discuss in a moment) and always has a plan in place for everything, which her bosses love her for, giving her a strong path of career advancement. Mary can always be counted on when it comes to planning and organizing an event and keeping the office running smoothly. She has creative ideas of her own, but thrives not in coming up with the idea, but orchestrating the plan behind its success. She tends to stay positive and upbeat but can sometimes get bogged down and anti-social when she feels overwhelmed. In terms of appearance, Mary is considered short, medium build, maybe slightly overweight by societal standards (but you're going to learn how to dismiss those in this book, so stay tuned), but she doesn't look it due to her medium build. She avoids eating heavy foods in excess because she feels like she can look at a piece of lasagna and gain five pounds just by seeing it. Mary will never be gaunt and willowy in frame and will never have a thigh gap, but she is considered attractive and has both a charismatic and commanding presence that garners respect and praise everywhere she goes.

Mary's coworker Jack is pretty much the opposite. Jack's elemental composition is predominantly air and fire elements. He is super tall and very slender. Jack is rather comedic, never has a plan in place, and prefers to come up with creative ideas on the spot and run with them or, more appropriately, create the ideas then let other people run with them. Jack can eat whatever he wants without gaining a pound, but his stamina tends to run out early, making him unfocused, forgetful, and unproductive towards the end of the day, much to the chagrin of his coworkers. Jack always has the best ideas in the weekly brainstorming session but will never be the one to follow through on them. Jack loves running as a form of exercise and stays extremely active. He's the life of the party, always has a boisterous energy and enthusiasm, and is someone who is friends with just about everyone, regardless of their personality or beliefs. Jack thrives on being social, creative, and getting along with everyone, whereas Mary thrives on ensuring the pieces all fit and work well together.

Jack and Mary are both very gifted but in very different ways. When Jack and Mary work together, they create amazing things.

If Jack were left to the details, he would likely fail, as would Mary if she had to be the visionary of the concept or the person selling the idea. We are like both Jack and Mary. When push comes to shove, you'll probably be able to do anything you put your mind to, but you definitely have your own unique talents and gifts that make you happy when you use them. And when you try to constantly push the river and do things that don't use your talents wisely (like Jack, when tasked with the details or Mary, when trying to be a social butterfly), you'll find yourself stressed out and unfulfilled. Maybe even sick.

Knowing your elemental type is one of the best ways to hone in on your unique talents and strengths, and also those things that you perceive to be weaknesses. This is the first part of the picture needed to understand your purpose in life, because those gifts and talents were given to you so you can use them in fulfilling your purpose, finding meaning, being happy, and maintaining good health. The more you know about how to take care of yourself based on your elemental type, the easier it becomes to live your purpose once you know what it is.

If you know you are the sort of person who doesn't have a high stamina, you'll have to pace yourself accordingly in order to succeed. If you know you're the sort of person whose composition makes them prone to having lots of energy and vitality, you'll make different choices for your lifestyle than the person in the opposite position. Just like if you know you're prone to gaining weight easily, you'll make different dietary choices than the person who can eat everything in sight and never gain a pound. Every physical trait has a corresponding personality trait that balances it out. Many people see gaining weight (or the propensity to) as a bad thing. I don't, and here is why. While earthy and watery people gain weight easily, they are also great builders, orchestrators, and people with great endurance and follow through. It's the same energy at play: builders can take formless energy and ideas and make substance out of it. Just like they can take food and make substance out of it in terms of their physical build. Super airy people will have to work much harder at gaining weight, but they also have to work that much harder to build the endurance and stamina to follow through on ideas and plans and change them from an idea to a reality.

It's important when understanding elemental differences to not cast judgement on anything and to understand that every perceived gift also comes with a perceived flaw. A great strength will always equal out to a great flaw in something else because that's how the universe works. When you cast judgement on someone for having a flaw, that means you likely do not see your own flaws or lack perspective. It also means that you're letting your differences divide you instead of unite you. My goal in outlining how the elements affect personality is so that you can learn to use your strengths in a way that enables you to minimize your weaknesses. No person really has an advantage over anyone else: when you know how to use what you're born with, the playing field is equal for everyone in terms of ability and raw talent.

Take a look at the diagram above and come up with three things you perceive as flaws in your life. Now find the counterbalance to it that you've learned in this chapter. When you find the strength that pairs with your perceived weakness, you'll learn how you can minimize the weakness so it doesn't control your life.

Let's use body shape and weight as an example, since body image is a huge part of self-esteem and confidence. We are going to use weight gain as a perceived flaw, although I don't believe it's a flaw at all. It's all a matter of perception, as you'll see.

Figure 1-3: perceived flaws & their corresponding gifts.

Perceived Flaw	Corresponding Gift
Easy weight gain.	Turns energy into tangible things.
Irritable or angry at times.	Ability to have strong focus and willpower.
Very emotional.	Compassionate and caring nature.
Perfectionistic.	Detail and precision-oriented.
Lacks follow-through.	Good ideas and creative side.
Not a social butterfly.	Time and space with your own thoughts.
Quiet and introverted.	Good at listening to people.
Needs validation of others.	Understands connections to other people.
Dislike of vigorous activity.	Inclined to activities like yoga or tai chi.
Talks too much.	Good at communicating thoughts and ideas.
Low stamina.	Knows how to pace oneself properly.
Doesn't party to have fun.	Understands how to set healthy boundaries.

Perceived flaw: I gain weight easily and, as such, weigh more than I want.

Counterbalance strengths: I have more endurance and stamina than many people. I see things through to completion. I have the ability to manifest things quickly and easily.

What does your strength equate to in real life? Let's take a look:

Real-life attributes of your strength:

- I can walk two miles a day and still have the energy I need for everything else in my day.
- I can eat lighter foods and still have sustained energy throughout the day.

- I can get more done in my job than others and have energy to focus on my personal life too.
- People can rely on me because they know I'll be there to see things through.
- Being there for others and knowing they can trust me is deeply fulfilling and helps me be happy.
- I can manifest things more easily than most people and know how to take an idea and make it a reality.

And the list goes on and on. Make it as long as you can! You can find ways to leverage each of these benefits to minimize your perceived weakness, which in this example was gaining weight easily. Walking two miles a day without a depletion in energy levels can keep your ability to gain weight in check. Eating lighter foods and having lots of energy from it can keep weight in check. Feeling good about yourself because you know you are dependable means you're not going to look to food for emotional comfort. You already have everything you need to succeed and to conquer your perceived flaw. God never gives you something you can't handle because you were created in the image of divinity itself. If there is something in your life that you have not yet conquered, find all of its corresponding strengths and let them be your fuel to succeed.

This is all an exercise in perspective, because without perspective it's impossible to have gratitude, compassion, or really feel good about yourself. Nothing is one-sided. Learn to see all situations and experiences in life from different points of view. It really upsets me when people say, "Have gratitude," as if that fixes everything, or, "You should be grateful for your life." Life is never a matter of "should," and gratitude is not something that can be cultivated just by looking at the good things around you. If that were the case, then you'd feel ungrateful when you see bad things or negative situations, which misses the point all together. Genuine gratitude comes from perspective—understanding both the good and bad of a situation and learning how to overcome the bad by way of the inherently good things you already have.

Here's the truth about you: you have the choice to see yourself as something remarkable or as something flawed. Both are undoubtedly true based on how you argue the logic behind it. But logic doesn't tell a story and doesn't have a start or an endpoint. It's merely a statement of facts that lacks soul, intention, and purpose. When you weave together your purpose with everything that makes you uniquely you (because remember, your purpose *is* what made you uniquely you), you become a story to be told, and you get to choose if your strengths or your weaknesses prevail. It's your story that puts the pieces together and gives meaning to all those inconsequential facts. The narrative is yours. Choose how you want to write it.

Breaking Through Societal Norms & Family Expectations

Understanding your inherent gifts and how to use them to maximize your strengths and minimize your weaknesses is the most important inner hurdle you'll face on your journey towards being uniquely you. But there is another important factor to consider: your external environment, including the thoughts and opinions of others.

How much emphasis you put on familial or societal expectations about your life depends a lot on the culture you were brought up in, how your family taught you to believe, and the people you currently spend the most time with. At the end of the day, it doesn't matter what potential you have or who you really are; what matters is what you believe about yourself and your own potential, no matter how true or untrue those beliefs are. And where do those beliefs come from? From what other people tell us. Let's look at the story of the elephant as an example.

A baby elephant in a circus has a small shackle around its leg, chaining it to a post so it can't escape. Each day the elephant is shackled so it can't run away, and as such, the elephant learns that the shackle prevents it from leaving. The elephant gradually becomes an adult, but the same small shackle is used to bind the elephant. The adult elephant can easily break the small shackle, but because the elephant has been habituated to believe it's trapped, it never tries to break free. It believes it's shackled and can't escape from its situation, and that becomes the elephant's story because the elephant doesn't know it can write another narrative for its life. The elephant truly believes it's powerless; even though you and I know that's completely untrue, the elephant's belief in itself is what dictates its actions and therefore its life.

The narrative we write for our own lives is always influenced by the people we spend the most time with, by our families, by our beliefs, and by societal norms. There is no way to avoid this because we are communal creatures, and we seek love and validation from others. But we *can* learn to overwrite external influences. The love a parent shows a newborn baby is what helps that baby grow and thrive. As a child, you don't have the discernment necessary to understand that what you're being taught may or may not be in your best interest. You're not expected to know any of that as a child, nor should you. Because children are so innocent and see the world through the eyes of love and without knowledge that people are truly capable of being bad or doing things to intentionally hurt others, we've all had experiences and learned lessons that are not in our best interest. These things need to be unlearned if you are going to continue to grow and become a better person. You can't choose your family, what happened to you, or what you were taught to believe or value growing up, but you can definitely choose what you continue to believe and value as you become an adult.

I grew up in a progressive family and was told I could be anything I wanted to be and do anything I wanted to with my life. I had my share of difficulties too (like having to deal with sexual abuse), but knowing I could use my potential any way I saw fit caused me to make some bold decisions and take chances in my life that other people wouldn't be willing to. Keep in mind, I grew up in a Western-minded household, which by default values individuality first and familial needs second. People grow up, get married, and start their own households. Single family households, typically, and that is definitely a Western concept. What about those who grow up in cultures where family and societal values are the priority and individuality is pushed to the back burner? Where households are multi-generational and you're always surrounded by the opinions and rules of others, especially your elders?

This is a very philosophical and spiritual topic, and one that deserves a lot of introspection. There is no definitive right or wrong in life: what you believe to be right or wrong is based on what you've been taught and habituated to believe over time. Things that are habitual and constant are things we become comfortable with, and comfort is a primary indicator, psychologically, of what we feel is right or wrong. Right or wrong is not based on what is actually right or wrong, it's based on how comfortable you are with something. We learn from the values and experiences of others because it forms a basis for us to understand life before we are able to gain our own experiences. But that doesn't mean that what you've learned is really who you are, what is right, or what is in your best interest to perpetuate.

Every self-governing person has to reevaluate their beliefs and lifestyle at some point: do you believe what you believe because you were taught to believe it and it's become the norm you're comfortable with? Or is it because your own life experience has given you perspective and repeatedly validated it to be true? This process of self-inquiry is a start to mindful living, because mindfulness relies on being conscious and present while not relying on input from habitual responses or feelings. Many people don't start this sort of introspective journey until awakening to a spiritual path or facing a mid-life or early-life crisis, and that's unfortunate because mindfulness is practically a prerequisite for a successful and happy life.

Psychological and emotional growth happens by gaining perspective and seeing different points of view. By hanging out with people from different cultures and belief systems. By expanding your horizons and trying new things. The most adept and wise people I know (not to mention by far the most interesting) are the ones who had great challenges growing up. Domineering families. Difficulties. Abuse. The ones who were made to live with difficulty and who ultimately had the courage and strength to become their own people despite how they were brought up. The obstacles were their fuel and a catalyst for gaining perspective and consciously choosing another way of living. This is what I call character development, and these are the type of people I respect and seek to spend time with.

Being uniquely yourself is extremely difficult when you come from a culture that de-prioritizes individuality or when you come from a challenging upbringing, but it's also necessary to have obstacles and difficulties if you really want to have perspective. Strength doesn't come by lifting light things. It comes by constantly challenging yourself to carry more weight. In life, perspective doesn't come from things being easy; it comes from enduring difficulties, learning there is always choice, and learning there is no absolute right or wrong.

It's literally impossible to know who you really are when you don't have perspective in life and don't challenge your current beliefs. You can gain tremendous wisdom and insight from others and from what you have been taught, and you should. But remember, what you've learned is only one viewpoint. One narrative. Perspective comes from having multiple points of view and vantage points into a situation. You should always challenge your current beliefs, because anything that is real will continue to be real, but the false perceptions you've held on to will start to slip away, making room for the person you have the potential to become. This doesn't mean old beliefs go away without a fight. New experiences will always cause some level of discomfort, otherwise you're probably not human. But new experiences also become the start of new traditions and a new habitual way of thinking that you'll grow comfortable with over time.

Until you combine perspective with your unique elemental type and everything that makes you unique as an individual, you won't fully know who you are. It takes both to have a good understanding of what makes you uniquely you. So the next time you feel bad about what you've experienced in life, the difficulties, struggles, or challenges, take a moment to realize those challenges are a huge gift that has been given to you so that you could gain the perspective necessary to understand who you really are. Your external environment and life experiences are the greatest tool you have for understanding who you really are, that is, when you realize you have a choice in who and what you become. That you're not the narrative someone else has written for you, or the shackled baby elephant, but the story of your own choosing.

People who follow the wishes and desires of others are never happy themselves, and there is a clear reason for this. If you were meant to live someone else's dreams, you would have been born as them and not yourself. You were born as you because you have something important to contribute to the world, and knowing yourself fully is the first step in that direction. We will talk more about being uniquely you and how to cultivate this in day-to-day life in Part II when we discuss mindfulness.

CHAPTER 2

INNER PROSPERITY & THE POWER OF FAITH

What is Inner Prosperity?

This may just be one of my favorite chapters of this book, because I love the concept of inner prosperity. It's the fuel that you need to succeed in life, stay healthy, and fulfill your purpose. Inner prosperity is a term I coined early in my journey to encapsulate the experience of what it means to be on the right path and be full of positive, vibrant, high-frequency energy. It's a tangible experience, yet it comes from a combination of things that are not tangible at all, making it the essence of things unseen, yet profoundly impactful in day-to-day life.

Inner prosperity itself is not directly measurable, just like faith, hope, or love are not measurable in and of themselves. You can't directly measure love or prove it exists, but you can clearly see its effects, and it's pretty much impossible to deny that it exists. Love even has measurable effects on the physical body. The evidence of inner prosperity's existence is seen in self-confidence, inner-peace, energy and vitality, staying healthy, being able to maintain a positive mindset, and radiating true charisma. It's palpable. You can see it and feel it in people in an undeniable way, and you'll be drawn towards people who radiate this presence. Inner prosperity *is* presence: it's when the essence of your soul is so perfectly aligned with your unique elemental constitution that a synergy is produced, making the sum greater than its parts. No aspect of yourself is diminishing your own light. Everything acts together to make your light shine even more brightly. Inner prosperity not only helps you fulfill your purpose for living, it's created by aligning powerfully with all of those aspects of yourself that were created from your purpose in the first place.

To me, inner prosperity is pure magic, or at least as close to magic as can be evidenced in day-to-day life. It's taking something without form and giving it substance through the positive outcomes it manifests in people's lives. Because of this, I see it as a definitive link between spirituality and health, with the causal seed of inner prosperity being purpose itself. It's a source of fuel we can use to keep mindset, spirituality, and even our physical bodies strong and full of vitality. This idea of taking something formless and using it to create form and substance may be hard to grasp, but we do it every time we take an idea and turn it into a reality.

Everything starts from the place of merely being an idea. A notion. An energy. Our work and effort are what take this energy and make it something real. We also do the opposite of taking something tangible and turning it into pure energy every day when we eat food. The body digests this food and breaks it down into energy, which is something intangible. The energy and nutrients we get from food act to sustain us physically, emotionally, and even mentally; it's not the original food itself, but the unseen energy and nutrients that come from it. Whether going from a solid to an energy or from an energy to something tangible and manifest, you can see it's the core energy we need to survive and thrive. We don't need the food directly, but the byproduct or fuel that comes from it. And let's not forget why we have this fuel to begin with. It's so we can use it to create meaningful things that are solid, measurable, and tangible in life. Things like a home. A caring family. A career that you love. None of this is possible without the subtle fuel of inner prosperity in our lives. Inner prosperity is a fuel and serendipitous catalyst that is created from purpose, used to bring us even closer to purpose and fulfillment in life. You could call it the energetic manifestation of purpose. How cool is that?

Let's take a moment to look at some of the physical manifestations that inner prosperity creates in life. While it all starts in the unseen, inner prosperity creates very tangible real-life experiences of positivity, faith, and good health.

Figure 2-1: the signs and symptoms of inner prosperity.

Symptoms	Mild	Moderate	Intense
Mental	Even-keeled, clearheaded, good memory.	Optimistic, brimming with ideas and insight, positive outlook, vast perspective.	Very positive mindset, plans for best possible outcomes, ability to multitask and focus very effectively.
Emotional	Happy, unburdened, joyful, at ease with life.	Really happy, sees the positive in all situations, tries to cultivate joy in others, charismatic presence.	Doesn't see the negative in anything, draws people in with one's energy, full of love and support.
Spiritual	Keeps up with daily spiritual practice, feelings of being connected and safe.	Always feels completely safe supported and heard by God, feels connected to others and the planet, seeks to help others whenever possible.	Full acceptance for the way things are right now, sees the interconnection in all things, believes God will bring everything one wants.
Physical	Relaxed, good energy levels, well-functioning body.	Energetic, upbeat, strong immune system, rarely gets sick, healthy flora, physically active.	Rarely or never gets sick, always has energy for everything, very physically active.

Faith, Belief & Inner Prosperity

The key to cultivating inner prosperity is to focus more on the intangible aspects of life that you can't directly measure (things like faith, hope, love, spirituality, and joy) than on the things you can directly see and witness. Make these things your foundation, not aspects of life that are supplementary. The reason it's important to make these seemingly intangible things your foundation is because you're tapping into the powers of faith and belief, and through that you're defining what is possible in your life. This is how you learn how to take a mere idea and shape it into something extraordinary. As we discussed earlier, it's not the reality of who you are that is most important but what you believe about yourself and believe to be possible that is. Your faith and belief in yourself are the two most important factors that will shape the trajectory and outcome of your life.

People always underestimate their own potential and what they're capable of. It's human nature to believe yourself to be limited or flawed until you work on retraining your mindset (which we'll discuss more in the chapter on mindfulness and meditation). The truth is, you're not limited at all. With enough inner prosperity, practically anything is possible because you'll actually believe you can do anything you set out to accomplish. If you want to cultivate strong inner prosperity, look to your thoughts. What do you have faith in, and what do you believe?

Belief is something we cultivate based on evidence. Maybe that evidence is from our own direct experience, or maybe it's through what we've been taught from others. Faith, however, is not based on any tangible evidence at all. It comes straight from the heart and soul of a person. Faith is like a belief (in that it's something we believe to be real) but without the tangible proof or experience to validate it. One of my favorite Bible verses is where it says even if you have faith the size of a mustard seed (a.k.a. really, really small), you can move mountains. It's so profound and so true. The soul knows things the mind can't even begin to comprehend. Technically, your soul knows everything that ever has been or will be. It's connected to the source of consciousness itself and can tap into that universal knowledge when it's needed. It knows and expresses its knowing through feeling and intuition. This is very different from the mind, which expresses knowing through memorization or learning. The mind relies on belief, whereas the heart makes its decisions based on faith. When you have faith and know something in your heart to be true, even without the mind having a shred of tangible evidence to back it up, you're connected with the unlimited knowledge and positive potential of the universe. That's something that cannot steer you wrong because it taps into something much greater than the mind alone.

Whatever you can imagine your life to be, you have the possibility of creating it. Your only limitations are what you can envision for yourself and what you're willing to work for. Even if the mind can't explain why you feel a certain way, those feelings are rooted in something real. If you feel you are heading in a certain direction and can envision it, that's your soul's way of letting you know the universe, God, or whatever name you have for consciousness itself, has already granted its consent and blessing for what you want.

Strong faith is something that turns into belief over time, because the intangible eventually turns into things with shape and form. You'll see the evidence of your faith once you really start aligning with it and living based on it. If you require evidence, you lack faith. If you have faith, you'll find the evidence necessary to turn faith into belief. If you are the kind of person that needs validation through evidence and lacks the ability to have faith, explore why this is, because it will hinder you in your journey towards purpose and health. Working with the intangible is the foundation for sustained success because it keeps the mind-body-soul triad functioning in harmony: it keeps the mind in check through the constant reminder that the most valuable things in life aren't based on belief but are felt through the heart. You can work with this unseen energetic essence through faith, visualization, meditation, mindfulness, love, or spirituality. Any of these will help nourish your soul with inner prosperity.

God, Religion & Spirituality

This is a good time to talk about God and what God represents to us psychologically, emotionally, and spirituality, while looking at the difference between spirituality and religion. The concept of God is seemingly the opposite of what it means to be human. God is considered perfect, unlimited, omnipresent, and omnipotent. It inspires faith to know there is a presence we can connect with that is capable of helping us navigate the difficulties of life. Faith in your connection with God is the wildcard for success: it's the only force we believe can do anything—even perform miracles. By connecting yourself with the unlimited power and possibility of God, you can overcome the limitations of the mind that make you believe you can't do something. God, and more specifically faith in God, gives you the keys of possibility to unlock your unlimited potential.

Faith in God is a major key to growing inner prosperity. How good you feel about yourself and your potential have a lot to do with how connected with God you believe you are. Do you believe you are always protected and looked over? Do you believe

God or the universe has your back at all times? Faith erases fear, and fear depletes inner prosperity. Fear is actually a major contributing factor to inner poverty.

Some people worship God because they believe themselves to be sinners in need of redemption. They need to feel loved because they cannot confront their own darkness and deeply love themselves. This notion of lack—the sinner mentality—is the basis of many religions, and that is unfortunate because the notion of feeling you inherently lack something is the basis of inner poverty (the opposite of inner prosperity). Others seek to unite with the unlimited potential that God represents—not to seek forgiveness for being unworthy but to walk in the image of our creator already fully worthy of grace and blessings. This is what I call spirituality. People can cultivate a spiritual connection through religion, but the connection you have with God, the universe, or whatever name you give to it is always personal and unique to you. Religion is about belief in God and following a doctrine of rules that determine your afterlife, whereas spirituality is about experiencing your personal connection with God directly, which impacts both your life now and what happens when you leave your body.

However you come to this place of feeling worthy, loved, and accepted by God, do it. Believing that you are worthy, and that unlimited potential and positivity is your birthright, is the key to cultivating inner prosperity.

The Spiritual Basis for Your Life's Purpose & Building Inner Prosperity

Earlier, I mentioned that inner prosperity is created from purpose and is also used to fuel your purpose in life. That seems mysterious, right? Let's look at this in a bit more detail. Looking at life from a spiritual perspective, we get to see how a mere idea or thought is taken and shaped into a tangible reality. Long before you were born, your soul—that unchanging, unperishable part of you—had something that it wanted to accomplish and experience by being alive. In order for this idea to manifest itself, the soul needed to clothe and adorn itself in a physical body gifted with the attributes and talents necessary to make the idea a reality. Different religions and spiritual traditions believe different things. People who believe in reincarnation often believe that the soul takes birth to experience life in many different ways, necessitating a different temperament and body type each time for all of these different lessons to be learned. If you believe we only take birth once, the core spiritual basis is still the same: God loves you so much that God has given you everything you need to succeed with your purpose in your core elemental composition and temperament. Because those are just fancy tangible frameworks that embody the specific energy types you need to be successful.

Your soul knows what you want to accomplish and what will make you happiest, so you are given the body and temperament type necessary to live a happy and fulfilled life. The body is like the clothing and adornment of the soul. When the soul works together with your unique body type, you can accomplish great things and stay in good health. This is the basic synergy that creates inner prosperity in life. You can build inner prosperity in many other ways, but this soul-body synergy is the basis and self-generating mechanism of inner prosperity that requires no additional effort on your part. Just like your body creates and uses metabolic energy daily to keep you going without a thought, your soul and body working together daily creates a similar baseline of energy called inner prosperity. When your soul and body function in harmony, you are naturally on the path towards living your purpose, whether you realize it or not.

If you're living in a way that doesn't throw the soul and body out of harmony, you'll have enough inner prosperity to live in balance. But this is modern life, abundant with stress, burnout, crazy work schedules, processed foods and poor diet choices, and so many other problems that functioning on this baseline of inner prosperity alone is nearly impossible. This is why we look to the spiritual basis of life as a way to build our stores of inner prosperity. When you tap into the wildcard that faith offers, you can bypass a ton of stress, you won't overly question everything in life (or at least not the things you know the mind will never find answers to), and you prime your mindset for positivity and success. Maybe you even meditate or have a mindfulness routine, daily prayer or worship, a mantra, an affirmation practice, or other things in your lifestyle that help cultivate your spiritual connection. Having a daily spiritual practice and things that reaffirm your faith ensure that your levels of inner prosperity stay well above the baseline needed to function and give you that necessary boost we all need to keep pushing forward, to deal with challenges, and to try new things.

When you drop below the necessary baseline of inner prosperity, this is when stress, health problems, anxiety, burnout, and more start to pop up. Instead of looking at these health and well-being challenges as problems, look at them as warning signs that show you the way back home. Look at depleted inner prosperity (which can manifest as inner poverty) as the first warning we get that shows we need to make changes in life to realign with our purpose. In order to stay happy, healthy, and live our purpose, we need that inner fuel. When it's depleted, you can be sure something in your lifestyle needs to be adjusted.

Using Purpose to Fuel Inner Prosperity

We often get bogged down worrying about health and well-being and try to tackle it head-on, thinking that a tangible problem requires a tangible solution to fix it. Instead of thinking of this solely in terms of the physical body, let's look at health and well-being through the lens of spirituality as a way to start tackling the problem, since your spiritual connection is at the root of cultivating inner prosperity. Remember, that basis of spirituality is in those things you can't see; not the tangible things you can. When you realize that inner prosperity is being depleted and you feel empty or downright ill, what can you change in your life that helps bring you back to your sense of purpose?

Ask yourself, why do I feel depleted? Did I work a ten-hour shift today which caused me to miss my daily walk and meditation time? (Note: working a ten-hour shift is fine but not when you sacrifice your spiritual connection for it.) Did I deprioritize myself because plans got changed? Did I allow someone to embarrass me today without standing up for myself? These seemingly small things add up to a mountain of burdens. And these small things will always bother you more when you push aside your spiritual practice to focus on the mundane and material. These things will bother you and deplete inner prosperity because they take you out of alignment with your purpose and highest potential; feeling troubled is a natural symptom of that. Nothing is coincidental.

One of the beautiful things about inner prosperity is that it acts as a shield against negativity and stress, and a little goes a long way. Without this shield, you become vulnerable and weak, emotionally and sometimes even physically. With this shield, you can push through difficulties and accomplish much more and let negative or stressful situations diffuse more quickly.

Emotions, stress, and anxiety are now well-known contributors to physical health problems, acknowledged by both scientific and medical communities. By working to change the way you feel through strengthening your faith, spiritual connection, and your connection and confidence in yourself, you create more inner prosperity in life, which can have a profound impact on your overall well-being.

Since inner prosperity and inner poverty are subtle things, let's look at some benchmarks in life to help you gauge your level of inner prosperity and see how full your tank is or determine if you've moved over to the spectrum of inner poverty.

What Exactly Is Inner Poverty?

I don't like talking about inner poverty, because focusing on it doesn't help you to fix it. As people, we have a tendency to focus more on what is bad than good, and this causes problems when all you need to do to start fixing things is to focus on building inner prosperity. With that in mind, let's just look at a couple pieces of key information so you can go back to focusing on the good in life.

Inner poverty can be considered the opposite of inner prosperity. It starts to happen when you drop below the baseline of inner prosperity needed for mind, body, and soul to function in harmony. In and of itself, it's only a lack of inner prosperity, so building more inner prosperity will fix the root problem. The real problem that comes into play is how long you feel in a state of inner poverty for. Whenever the mind gets used to a certain way of feeling and being, neural connections form, which make this your new normal. Rewiring those neural connections takes consistency and time to adopt a new behavior, belief, and routine. We will discuss this in more depth in the chapter about mindfulness.

If you notice yourself becoming depleted and quickly act to reverse those effects (like taking a relaxing bath at the end of a stressful day), you won't form a habitual state of inner poverty. If you let the problems build up and keep pushing your well-being aside, that's when the real problems begin.

Figure 2-2: signs & symptoms of inner poverty.

Symptoms	Mild	Moderate	Severe
Mental	Stress, feeling overwhelmed, lack of focus, unclear of what's important and not.	Depression, anxiety, memory problems, lack of clear path to follow.	Burnout, believes there are not new opportunities, brain fog, and confusion.
Emotional	Sadness, failure to stand up for one's self, putting other people's needs first, self-doubt.	Inability to thrive, pessimism or lack of optimism, numbness to some feelings.	Negative viewpoint of life, belief that worst is deserved, not allowing for happiness, anger, jadedness and apathy towards self or others.
Spiritual	Skipping daily prayer or worship, skipping self-care.	Disconnection from God, belief God isn't listening or doesn't care, feelings of being adrift, lack of a plan.	Anger with God, propensity to blame God for problems.
Physical	Sluggishness, fatigue, low energy.	Headaches, anger, emotional outbursts, declining health or presence of illness, beginning of chronic conditions.	Imbalance in gut flora, physical illness or chronic health condition, pain.

Ditch Inner Poverty & Get Back to Inner Prosperity

The quickest way to get back on track is through your spiritual connection and through adequate self-care. Take time for yourself each day for your spiritual practice and make your emotional well-being a priority. This in and of itself nips inner poverty in the bud and helps to restore your vitality and inner prosperity. In the next chapter, you'll learn an entire framework for well-being with The WELL Method. For now, let's look at three specific things you can do to get back on track.

Step 1 – The Five Sense Check-in
Step 2 – Commit to one daily consistent routine that makes you happy and is just for you
Step 3 – Enliven your spiritual connection

I've found it's the simple things in life done consistently that leave the biggest impact. If you find yourself in a place of inner poverty, hit your internal reset button. Start by doing a Five Sense Check-in. Take one to two minutes to quickly evaluate what's happening with each of your five senses. In this very moment, what is it that you smell, taste, see, feel, and hear? Take twenty seconds on each sense to really tune in and see what you are perceiving with each one. Maybe you have the taste in your mouth of the last thing you ate during lunch. Maybe you smell rain or the smell of smoke coming from a nearby fireplace or grill. Perhaps your skin feels cold, and you realize you need to wrap up in a blanket. Check in with each sense and see what is going on. This is a powerful way to come back to the present moment and out of a place of thought. Your five senses connect to the five elements and also connect you directly with your feelings. Once you have a grasp on what is happening with each of the senses, tune in to what you're feeling and see if any of your feelings are connected to anything you're experiencing through the senses.

Next, tune into your emotions and identify at least one thing, one experience, you've been missing in your life that used to bring you joy. This is always easiest to do after a sensory check-in because you get the mind out of the way and are in a place of perceiving through your feelings and not the mind. Note, the thing you've been missing is not a person. It's not an old boyfriend or girlfriend. It's not a powerful memory back to a time you were happy but cannot relive. It's something that is immediately within your control to change—something you've deprioritized or put on the back burner due to the busyness of life.

Don't use this as an excuse to wallow in self-pity or focus on what you're lacking; use it to identify something that you have full control over that you've been neglecting. It's highly likely that you've stopped doing something that you enjoy, whether that's as simple as a daily walk, morning prayer, a cup of tea each afternoon, or a quick call to a good friend each night. Maybe it's working out, singing, or dancing. Maybe it's something downright silly. Whatever it is, make the commitment to restart this behavior immediately. Now, put this book down and go do that thing you've been missing! There's no time like now.

Let's say you can't identify anything that's missing. Focus on creating a new positive habit that you can do each day. This brings us to the second technique to ditch inner poverty: cultivate a consistent daily habit that makes you happy. Maybe you didn't realize how much that cup of tea each day really did for you. That's normal. People almost always underestimate how much small things have a major impact on how you feel. Now is the time to change this.

When making a new daily habit, make sure it's something that makes you feel warm and fuzzy inside. Not something that you think you should be doing, like meditation or exercise, and not something that will allow you to multitask. This exercise is different. This is about making time for you each day to feel good about yourself (yay for putting yourself first!) and forming a new behavior that will help rewire the neural connections in your brain to something positive. My daily habit starts with a cup of tea each morning, either alone or with a close friend. Rain or shine, staying in or heading to work or the gym, it doesn't matter. My day always begins with a cup of tea! You'll know you're on track to finding your routine when it seems frivolous or inconsequential. You have my assurance that it's not. It may, in fact, be one of the single most important things you do to keep inner prosperity on track and inner poverty out of sight.

Step three is to enliven your spiritual connection. You probably would have thought this would be step one or two. It's not any less important, but doing these three things in order will lead to the best results. Life can get crazy sometimes, so it's important to prime the mind and senses to be fully present before we start to focus on our spiritual connection. When you're fully centered, you can have the best experience, no matter what way you relate to your highest self and God. A spiritual connection can mean very different things. For some people, it's spending time in prayer, for others it's worship or song, for some it's spending time at church or temple, and for others it's doing rituals or pujas that help them connect. Whatever your unique combination is, make time for it.

A decline in inner prosperity almost always begins by neglecting our daily routines, spiritual or otherwise. It's subtle at first, and you may not even notice until problems arise, like stress or fatigue. If you don't have a consistent daily spiritual routine, make one. Start off simple, so that you can stay consistent with it. Spirituality is one of those things we are meant to feel. If you aren't feeling the connection, find something that makes you come alive and feel connected. There are so many ways to worship and commune with God and your highest self that you are sure to find a way that works for you.

I'm very much into practical spirituality; for me, a strong connection is evidenced through day-to-day life. Can I give someone a compliment that improves their day? How can I show compassion and understanding when negative situations arise? How can I best forgive people who have caused pain? Am I making sure my words are kind or at least necessary? Am I using money and material possessions in the best way possible without being wasteful? Am I relating to my sexuality in a way that leaves me feeling sacred, connected to God, and fulfilled as an individual? Am I using my power to make the lives of other people better? If I'm not doing these things, it's a warning sign for me that my spiritual connection is off-balance. How do you live your spirituality in day-to-day life? What are the tangible things you do differently when you feel supported and loved by God?

While we need to have consistency in our spiritual practices, it's also good to freshen things up from time to time. We grow and change and, as such, our behaviors also need to grow and change, which includes the way we worship. Identify one new thing you can add to life that you feel will strengthen your spiritual connection, and give it a try for the next week. See how it goes, and be mindful that it takes time for the mind to adjust to new things. You may just find the next thing that makes you feel blissfully alive and awake.

CHAPTER 3

THE WELL METHOD

How The WELL Method Came into Existence

The WELL Method was born out of my need to recover my health and fulfill my purpose in life. When Western medicine failed me, I had no other choice but to find a way to heal my life naturally. I had so much to heal, not only physically but also some deep emotional wounds that affected my sense of self-worth. I felt completely emotionally and physically bankrupt—pretty much the definition of experiencing inner poverty.

I knew that healing had to be possible because God would not put me in an impossible situation; we are always set up to succeed, not fail. Even though I didn't know how I was going to move forward or get well when I began my journey, I knew that I would. I knew that somehow my purpose was connected to my health and well-being (or lack of it) and that there would be no way I could heal if I continued to feel emotionally bankrupt, meaning my emotions were also connected to my health and well-being.

Even though I've been healthy and fully pursuing my purpose for several years now, it was only recently that I developed The WELL Method, and I did so to share the profound connection I discovered between purpose and well-being. For a long time, I wasn't sure if what I did could be replicated by others. I mean, I have only known a handful of people to recover from a debilitating disease or crippling medical diagnosis, so it took me some time to figure out why that is. What was the actual focal point of why I got well? Why is it that two people do vastly similar things, and one of them gets better while the other doesn't? Finally, the answers dawned on me.

It's not as much about what a person does; it's about the mindset, motivation, and beliefs of a person before they begin and whether or not a person is committed to living their unique life's purpose. It's in the energy and idea phase that we determine the outcome, which is why we've looked closely at inner prosperity before discussing The WELL Method. Where is your head at? What do you have faith in? What is the inner dialogue you're having with yourself? What do you believe the outcome of the journey will be before you start? These things are what determine the outcome. I believe this is why I got well and is often why other people don't.

When health is looked at as separate from purpose, joy, and mindset, health is not possible. Where you start on your journey determines what your experience will be like, the lessons you'll need to learn to reach your desired outcome, and even where you'll end up if you don't change course. You cannot plot out the course until you know your starting point, and this starting point is all about your mindset, faith, and level of inner prosperity.

I created The WELL Method acronym to set people up for success from day one by creating a mindset of unlimited positive potential that you can shape to fit your own unique dreams and desires. Think of the acronym as your cornerstone for cultivating a wellness lifestyle that supports a happy, healthy, and purpose-driven life.

The WELL Method Acronym

W—Work-Life Harmony

E—Expect Excellence

L—Live Your Purpose

L—Love, not Fear

Everything that I'll teach you in this book will relate back to at least one of these core concepts and likely more than one at the same time. Just like mind, body, and spirit are three parts of the same whole, the four parts of The WELL Method are cornerstones to the foundation of a fulfilled, healthy life. The beauty in the acronym is that it works no matter what your definition of each cornerstone is or what your faith or belief system is. It gives you the ability to set personal goals that make you feel good about your life and your lifestyle. And remember, your definitions will grow and evolve as you grow and evolve as an individual, so there really is unlimited potential in what you envision your life to become. The key is to start with what makes sense to you and feels right for you now, in this moment.

W—Work-Life Harmony

Ultimately, we all want work-life balance and fulfillment in both career and personal life, even though that concept will mean different things to different people. Note that I call this work-life harmony and not work-life balance because balance refers to a juggling act, and that's not a positive way to view your life. Life shouldn't be about juggling; it should be about creating beauty, just as harmony does in music. When the pieces of life work together in harmony, you create synergy. You create something that is more than the sum of its parts, and that creates meaning in life. It's a completely different perspective; viewing life through the lens of harmony will help build inner prosperity.

Even if your work is as a full-time mom or caregiver to someone else or another situation where you're not being monetarily compensated for your time or efforts (bartering, retirement, etc.), it's still work if you're putting consistent time and energy into it. For one person, work-life harmony may mean cultivating a career where you're not trading time for money, whereas to another person, it may mean setting healthy boundaries between a full-time job, family responsibilities, and personal passion projects. The beauty is that you can find what works for you while still having a positive and constantly evolving goal to work towards.

The key to success with work-life harmony is to understand what is important to you right now in your life and to be able to advocate for this with your spouse, employer, and other people you're working and interacting with. Many companies have flexible work policies, so as long as you are clear with your goals and your manager is clear about what's important to you, you can work towards getting the time and or space you need to succeed. I've worked as a manager for many years, and the employees who were clear with me about their needs always got them met. Unfortunately, most people never knew what they wanted and therefore didn't ask. They didn't take time to know what was valuable to them, other than compensation and vacation time. When it comes to your spouse (if you have one), they likely want to see you happy, and having clear expectations will help your relationship thrive. When you know your goals and can ask for them, people will usually work with you. Having clarity about what you want makes it possible to get what you want. It's also a great benchmark for fulfillment when you can create clear goals and work towards accomplishing them.

E—Expect Excellence

The second cornerstone, expect excellence, is closely connected to inner prosperity and positive mindset. By expect excellence, I literally mean to expect that you will succeed in all things you put your mind and heart to. This may start off as a belief to you, but my hope is that it evolves into an inner knowing (or gnowing, referring to *gnosis*) that life is so perfect—and that you've been created so perfectly—that you have everything inside yourself that you need to succeed. It's merely a matter of positioning yourself for the success you were born to have by strengthening your talents and minimizing your weaknesses. People with strong inner prosperity will always expect excellence of themselves because they realize that what happens in life is in large part based on desire and hard work.

Part of expecting excellence from yourself is dependent on having the right mindset and motivation to succeed. Not only do you need clear goals if you are to accomplish them, you need a clear plan in place to cultivate mindfulness and a positive perspective on life. We will discuss specific mindfulness and meditation approaches later in this book, as well as the direct connection between food and mood (spoiler: certain foods directly stimulate neurotransmitters in the body that produce our "feel good" hormones), so for now let's focus on the conceptual piece.

It's possible and attainable to expect excellence of yourself each and every day of your life. It's not possible or attainable to always be in a good mood or to be perfect though. Make sure you know the difference between having the mindset to strive for great things versus always getting them or feeling great. Our feelings and emotions are experienced so that we can live a full and meaningful life. It's the negative experiences we have and the negative feelings we experience like grief, sorrow, frustration, fear, and even anger that give us the perspective necessary to fully understand what happiness, joy, gratitude, and fulfillment are. Without perspective, you'd never really know. Without sorrow, you would not be able to define joy. Without feeling a sense of lack, you wouldn't know what it means to be fulfilled. Without experiencing the ugliness of life, how would you know what is beautiful?

Negative things don't happen to us to set us back. They happen so that we can be as happy and fulfilled as possible. As humans, we're very experiential creatures. We need to directly experience life if we are to learn its lessons and assimilate its knowledge, turning it into wisdom. Knowledge can be gained by learning from others, but wisdom is always a mark of personal experience. Negative experiences, when judged on their own, will lead to sorrow, but when we understand them in terms of the big picture of our whole and fulfilled life, they become just another brushstroke—a necessary brushstroke that provides contrast, illuminating the entire picture for us to see.

In order to expect excellence of yourself, you must be in this journey for the long haul. You can't get lost in the trees of minor setbacks and forget the rest of the forest. Look at the big picture first, then focus down on the smaller details and the daily situations and circumstances you find yourself in. The devil is most definitely in the details because if you focus too much on them or don't understand their connection to the larger picture, you'll get lost on your journey.

L—Live Your Purpose

Live your purpose is pretty direct, and by the end of this book you'll know how to discover and hone in on your purpose at any point in life and find ways to start living it, if you haven't already done so. Everything that's encapsulated in The WELL Method is in the birthright of every human being: we are all endowed with the same ability to accomplish our goals and live a purpose-driven life. And we all have the tools to discover what our purpose is and learn how our unique talents and gifts fit into our purpose.

You have all the tools you need to know your purpose, but you still have to make the time and space to do it and to live by the cornerstones and adapt them in day-to-day life. Living your purpose is not just something you wake up one day and decide to do. It's a bunch of small daily actions taken together that add up to something more profound that enables you to fulfill your purpose for living. It's so easy to let these small things go or push them to the back burner when life gets busy. It's all too easy to put your dreams on the back burner when trying to harmonize work, family, passion, and everything else you have going on in life. The cornerstone "live your purpose" is to remind you to prioritize your life to include the small and meaningful things that enable you to live your purpose. To remember to dream big and to know if you have the power to truly dream it, you can make it a reality.

L—Love, not Fear

Love, not fear is a perspective and mindset that enables you and the people around you to succeed. Fear-based decisions and actions look and feel much different than decisions and actions made from a place of love. Love is like a glue that unites all things; it brings diverse things and people together as one cohesive whole. Fear does the exact opposite; it uses our differences as a way to divide and split things or people apart. Living from a perspective of love is easy to do when you expect excellence from yourself and when you've cultivated strong inner prosperity. It's also easy when you acknowledge that God, consciousness, the universe, or whatever you call that unifying source energy, always functions from a place of love. The universe and consciousness as a whole always want to say yes to your desires! The universe sees life as a cohesive whole—a great web of life—even if we don't function from that mindset of love and unification. The law of karma is evidence of this, in that whatever it is you give to others or act like in life, the universe gives back to you. Because why, of course, would you treat others in a way you didn't want to be treated yourself?

Coming from a place of love means learning to see from other people's perspective. What's their situation? What is causing them to act the way they are acting? Here's an example. Say you're managing a team of employees, and one of them comes into work fifteen minutes late. How will you choose to respond to this? If from a place of fear, you'll likely criticize and punish the employee for being late because they broke your rule. In this situation, you've made the response about you and the rules, not them. It's come down to prioritizing a thing (in this instance a rule) over the real-life experience of a person and looking at a situation from a black-and-white perspective of right and wrong. Black-and-white anything is rooted in fear. If you choose to come from a place of love, you'll take the time to find out *why* your employee was late. Was the subway broken down or delayed? Did they have car problems? Did they oversleep? Was it beyond their immediate control? Remember, love connotes strong inner prosperity, and someone who feels love pouring out of them will always look for ways to continue to bless or forgive those around them. If the situation was not their fault, you'd likely give them a pass. If it was their fault, maybe you'd give them a pass anyway with a request to do better next time. No one is perfect, after all.

Life will always present you with situations that you get to either react to or respond to. Reaction comes from fear and not seeing the big picture. Response comes from seeing the whole situation and consciously choosing to act from a place of love. While this has an obvious connection to how we interact with others, it also has a major impact on our own lives because of how love impacts the mind. When you choose to respond to a situation instead of reacting to it, the mind becomes more fluid and expansive. You're paving the way for personal growth and expecting excellence of yourself. We'll talk more on this later in chapter 8.

Mind-Body-Soul—One Unified Consciousness

If you walk away from this book with one foundational piece of wisdom, let it be that mind, body, and soul are three parts of the same whole. This truly is foundational to understanding what wellness is and how to facilitate sustained well-being in life. There's even scientific evidence now to support how interconnected the mind, emotions, and body are to each other.

The soul, or spiritual side of our nature, is the one that, while we can't prove it exists, it's impossible for most of us to deny that it exists. It's that piece of you that gives you purpose, passion, and the knowledge that you're here for a reason. It's the piece of you that connects you with everyone and everything else in existence, and it's the piece that makes love so profound. Empathy, compassion, courage, the desire to help others, and a deep sense of purpose are all traits that are born from the connection we have to our soul.

How in touch we are with our soul is strongly connected to our emotional and mental states, and to how we process reality. People who are more connected to their soul and spiritual nature tend to live happier and more meaningful, purpose-driven lives. While the soul's connection to health is not tangible by itself, we now have hard-core science that shows our mood and emotions (which are strongly reliant on our spiritual connection) play a role in immune function and staying healthy. We've long known that a depressed or sad mood can have a negative impact on a person's mental state, but it's now also known that when you feel sad, depressed, angry, or any other negative emotion, it can affect whether you get physically sick or not. The more positive your mood, the stronger your immune system is likely to be. The more you feel sad or distressed, the weaker your immune system will likely be. This is the link between inner prosperity and health—happy, fulfilled people are healthier people, statistically speaking.

And let's not forget about mental health. Recent studies have shown that depression may be caused by inflammation in the brain and body and not solely due to chemical imbalance as previously thought, strongly supporting why foods like turmeric with strong anti-inflammatory properties can have a profound and positive effect on mood. Other studies have shown a correlation between healthy flora in the gut and healthy mental states. When the gut flora gets out of balance or depleted, this can trigger depression in people. These studies elucidate how when you take care of the physical body, you're helping to take care of the mind and emotions as well.

Exercise, which is primarily for the physical body, has long been known to play a role in positive mood in addition to physical health, and now we also know that foods can have a profound effect not only on our bodies but on our moods as well. By taking care of your mental health and moods, you're helping to support good health in the physical body, just as taking care of the physical body helps support positive mental health, moods, and emotions. This concept is far from new. Louise Hay was well known for teaching people the connection between their moods, emotions, and physical health problems, but having more and more scientific evidence every day that supports the interconnection makes these concepts approachable to more people.

Differences Between East/West Approaches to Wellness

The mind-body-spirit connection to health and wellness is the fundamental difference between Eastern approaches to wellness and the Western medical approach. You see, Western medicine believes that a disease or illness is the main problem and that in order to get healthy, you need to target the disease directly and kill it. Eastern approaches to wellness, including both traditional Chinese medicine and Ayurveda, have a completely different perspective. They believe that wellness and good health are an outcome of mind, body, and spirit balance. We're exposed to illnesses and disease constantly, but it's only when a person gets out of balance that a disease can take advantage of that imbalance and cause a problem for our health. When the body is in balance, that same disease does not have an entry point to manifest itself as a problem or grow into a full-fledged illness. In the Eastern approach, the imbalance is the problem, and not the disease itself.

Let's say you already have a disease or illness; by Eastern methodology, that would mean you have an imbalance between mind, body, and spirit. It's believed that regaining balance will enable the body's own healing mechanisms to kick in and destroy the disease because there is no longer an environment conducive for the illness to thrive in. The Western medical approach believes a disease won't go away until you target and kill it directly. This is because the Western medical approach does not have any framework for looking at a unified system that includes a soul or something outside of its ability to tangibly measure and account for.

It's fascinating because some insurance plans cover Eastern approaches like acupuncture, which are based in flow of chi or subtle energy (which you also cannot prove exists), but the positive effects are apparently enough evidence to validate this approach to wellness. I look forward to the day that mind-body-spirit wellness becomes the normal paradigm of health and people realize how fundamentally important it is to treat and take care of all facets of our being and our lives.

While we are talking about balance, I want to express how much I dislike that word and how misleading it can be. Let's just say it—balance is sterile and boring! Why would we want to strive for that? Mind, body, and soul balance, the way that phrase is traditionally used, does not mean that all three are in some sort of equilibrium or that each is equally weighted. It means that you are working with each facet to the best of your ability and that each of those three pieces of you are being prioritized in life in a way that makes you feel happy and fulfilled. Nothing is ever fully in balance. In fact, some spiritual texts say that if all the three *gunas* (different forms of energy) were in perfect balance, the universe would cease to exist. You are unique as a person, and your uniqueness means that mind, body, and soul will be prioritized differently than the person next to you. It will even vary for you based on where you are in your life. Focus on how healthy your mind, body, and soul are, not on balance. You'll find me getting away from the word balance and focusing more on the concept of fullness and inner prosperity. Inner prosperity is more clearly aligned with the positive outcomes we're all looking for. Even health itself is just a reflection of inner prosperity—how brightly you are shining and how fulfilled your life is on all fronts. You'll see why by the time you've finished this book.

To bring all of this together, mind, body, and soul are three different manifestations of the same whole, but instead of thinking about well-being as being about balance, let's look at it in terms of how fulfilled each piece is and how effectively each piece of you can work together as a synergistic whole being. This is the key right here. When well-being is based off of synergy, you don't have to focus on the negatives at all to make change in life. You don't even have to focus on "taking care" of the physical body as a means of staying healthy. If you take exceptional care of your mental, emotional, and spiritual self, you'll find the body is a part of that and that your physical body is healthy. When you work with mindset and emotions as your foundation, everything else falls into place naturally. When you make choices that benefit the whole you, the whole you benefits.

Inner Prosperity & The WELL Method

In order to show the connections between purpose and well-being, it's first important to understand the connections of inner prosperity to well-being, which is why we've covered this early on in the book. Inner prosperity, like purpose, is not a tangible, tactile thing. But both are part of the foundations of your fulfilled and healthy life.

When working with The WELL Method, inner prosperity plays a major role in each of the four cornerstones because it sets the stage for making positive personal goals that are meaningful to you. For a person lacking inner prosperity, it can be hard to set clear boundaries and communicate your goals clearly with others, which is necessary for cultivating the W: work-life harmony. It's even hard to know what is really important to you when you lack inner prosperity because of intrinsic feelings of unworthiness. The more inner prosperity you cultivate, the greater your sense of self-worth, confidence, and willingness to advocate for your needs and desires.

The second cornerstone, expect excellence, is really where you get to dive in and use inner prosperity as fuel to set attainable goals for yourself. Here are some of the ways I expect excellence out of myself: daily meditation, daily contemplation and mindfulness, daily exercise, and daily me-time. It's work, and some days, it's a real challenge. Excellence requires personal effort, but it's worth it because you're worth it. Cultivating consistent routines where you are growing and honing your skills, taking care of yourself, and constantly pushing yourself to do and be better means you have to have a positive mindset and lots of inner prosperity. The thing is, while you need inner prosperity to do these things to begin with, doing them helps build inner prosperity in life because you're doing things that'll make you feel good about yourself. Not only will you gain more inner prosperity through personal development, the more inner prosperity you cultivate, the more you will *want* to expect excellence of yourself. Pretty cool, huh?

Just to be perfectly clear on this, inner prosperity is fuel for expecting excellence in yourself, and it also is the fuel that creates the desire for you to want to work on yourself. There are no coincidences. As I've said, you were created perfectly and given everything that you need to succeed. This is just more evidence of it.

Living your purpose hinges on how successful you are with the first two cornerstones because you won't have the motivation or energy to live your purpose without work-life harmony and the amazing benefits you'll get from the consistent routines put in place to drive you closer to excellence. Consistency, motivation, positive mindset, and that underlying drive to succeed are what the W and E in The WELL Method provide. Living your purpose will come much more easily when these are in place. In the next chapter, we'll dive into purpose even more deeply and help you find out exactly what it is for you at this point in your life.

Living with love is something that you can and should practice cultivating, and it's also something that will come more naturally on its own when the W, E, and first L in The WELL Method are working for you. When things are in harmony and going well, you'll have more gratitude in life and be more apt to respond positively to others. Reaction comes when we're not fulfilled and when we don't feel that God is taking care of us. It stems from fear, and fear is always coming from a place of lack or pain. You can use the inner prosperity you're cultivating in life to stop your reaction patterns and speed up the other cornerstones of The WELL Method, and you'll also see less reactiveness and more responsiveness as a natural byproduct of living by the cornerstones of The WELL Method. It's all synergistic.

If you focus on cultivating any single cornerstone of The WELL Method, it will have a positive effect on each of the other cornerstones, making them all easier to accomplish. Each cornerstone has synergy with the other three, forming a solid foundation to live life from. For those of you into sacred geometry like me (I geek out on it sometimes), the four cornerstones form a square, just as the lotus petals of the first chakra do. Squares provide the most solid foundation possible that you can build anything on top of.

Set Your WELL Method Acronym Goals

Now that you know each of the four cornerstones of The WELL Method, it's time to set your personal goals and define what each pillar means to you, right here and right now. Keep in mind that your definitions will always grow, expand, and even change with time, so write down what is important to you right now. Note that I said what *is* important, not what *should be* important. There is a vast difference between the two.

As you continue this book, you'll learn more ways to fill in each of these sections and create an entire personalized plan to help you find your purpose, to live it each day, and to cultivate sustainable mental, emotional, and physical well-being while you do.

Figure 3-1: fill in the following diagram to the best of your ability. Be as clear & specific with each answer as you can.

W – Work Life Harmony	It is important for me to have these three things to feel that my career and personal life are fulfilling and not competing with each other: 1. 2. 3.
E – Expect Excellence	In order for me to expect excellence of myself, it's important that I do or honor these three things each day: 1. 2. 3.
L – Live Your Purpose	Living my purpose means that I must have strong inner prosperity. Doing these three things will keep my inner prosperity strong: 1. 2. 3.
L – Love, not Fear	Responding to situations is a conscious choice. Here are three things that enable me to respond to life and not react to it: 1. 2. 3.

CHAPTER 4

IDENTIFY YOUR PURPOSE & CREATE YOUR PURPOSE PLAN

Figuring out your life's purpose need not be difficult when you look at the two primary factors that fuel it. In the last chapter, you outlined some ideas for your personal WELL Method plan. You'll get more insight on that in the next section of this book. For now, let's dive into the primary factors that shape your purpose, learn what purpose is and is not, and begin creating your Purpose Plan.

Identify Your Purpose

Your unique elemental composition is factor number one. Early in chapter 1, we looked at the five elements and the attributes associated with each. You have an elemental composition that was determined by your life's purpose in order to give you the talents that you need to succeed. If you'd like to dive deeper into determining and understanding your personal elemental type, I highly recommend reading my book, *Vibrational Healing: Attain Balance & Wholeness. Understand Your Energetic Type.* It contains interactive quizzes to determine your exact elemental composition. If you'd like just a rudimentary breakdown of your primary elements, you'll learn how to figure that out in chapter 7. By determining your unique elemental breakdown, you'll start to understand your strengths and weaknesses and how they work together to create the masterpiece you are. The fun begins when you look at these attributes in combination with each other.

I'd like you to write out a list of your personal attributes (you can use Figure 1-2 as a reference for this), both your strengths and perceived weaknesses. Make a column for each. Now make another list of things you enjoy. This can be anything, from foods to arts to hobbies to possible career options. You will start to see overlap here between your attributes and the things you feel drawn to.

Figure 4-1: my personal strengths, weaknesses, and things that interest me. Use Figure 1-2 as a reference for identifying personal attributes.

Strengths	Weakness	Things I Enjoy or Am Interested In

Here's an example from Jane:

Strengths	Weakness	Things I Enjoy or Am Interested In
Organized	Nit-picky	Colors, textures and shapes interest me
Methodical	Hates exercise	Writing
Empathy	Often tired	Communicating with people through spoken conversation
Caring	Gets taken advantage of	Helping people
Go-Getter	Perfectionistic	Cooking and baking

See how in the list of attributes, Jane mentions organization and being methodical, and in the list of things she's drawn to, she puts colors and shapes? This pairing tells me that Jane could be an excellent interior designer. She has an innate talent for organizing things and an interest in the use of colors and shapes, which is essentially décor. With the right training, this could be a fulfilling career path. She could also be an architect, depending on whether her creative or methodical side is stronger. Jane also loves cooking, having conversations, and helping people. This suggests she's a good listener and would thrive in an environment where she gets to interact with people regularly, sharing her input and expertise—again, great for a designer. These skills could also be used in a counseling career, as a teacher or mentor, maybe even a program manager for a non-profit doing humanitarian work. I bet you can think of some career choices for Jane as well. The more you dive into how your attributes combine with your interests, you'll see there are so many different possibilities!

You're probably telling yourself this is awesome, but there are still too many things to choose from to know my purpose. You are right because this is only half of the picture. This brings us to factor number two: your personal life experience. We've all had experiences in life that shape us. Experiences that leave an extremely positive or negative impact. In fact, you've probably had both in your life. Both the good and bad experiences are blessings because they've made you who you are, and both should be used as fuel for finding your purpose.

While we all strive for joy and happiness, it's most often the painful situations we experience that are the most meaningful in shaping our trajectories. The pain in life drives humanity to make the world a better place so that others don't have to have the same bad experience. Or at least, so more people are able to find solace and healing from their emotional wounds afterwards. Physical wounds heal quickly, but emotional wounds can last a long time unless you consciously work to heal them. Helping others is one of the ways we help ourselves heal and move on. It completes the circle and can bring closure and meaning to the pain we've experienced.

Your most painful experiences can bring the deepest and most profound meaning to life when the residual emotions left behind are put to good use. Combine those with your best experiences, and you may well have an understanding of how you can best help others, while helping yourself and finding fulfillment. When you combine your unique talents (conferred from your elemental composition), your interests, and the emotions from your most impactful life experiences, good and bad, you have the perfect recipe for finding your path to purpose.

It's important to recognize that your purpose is not a fixed thing that is set for your entire life. Purpose is something that evolves and changes as you evolve and change. Since your life experiences account for half of what shapes your purpose, as you have more experiences and continue to grow as a person, your sense of purpose will also continue to grow and evolve. Your elemental composition won't change, but depending on which of your innate talents you choose to cultivate, and how you cultivate them, you will grow and change.

The more work you do to heal past emotional wounds, the less the emotions from those experiences will drive your sense of purpose. Deep wounds take time and effort to heal, and as they do, you may find your purpose changing. This is a good thing! It means that while you have the memory of your experience, you've healed the emotional piece so that it no longer drives your actions. Meaning is shifted to something else—another deeply held experience you've had whose emotional connection is still with you. Or maybe, you lean in more to your innate talents and choose to cultivate them in different ways. The possibilities are endless for how your purpose can manifest itself.

Adulting vs. Purpose

While we're talking about finding purpose, let's look at what it is not. I've heard so many people say, "My purpose is to be a good mom to my kids," or "My purpose is to get good grades and pursue my career." Let's stop right here. These things are *not y*our purpose because they are things that apply to anyone in that same situation. Being good at the things you give your time and energy to is what it means to expect excellence of yourself. These situations have nothing to do with what makes you unique and special as a person. Raising a healthy and stable family or doing what you need to support a good career is not purpose;

it's expecting excellence in yourself, and that is foundational to well-being for every person, regardless of what your purpose is.

I'm not saying you have to work or have kids (those were just common examples I used); whatever you do, give it your best. Expecting excellence in yourself is adulting 101, and it's part of the societal norm of what life looks like, but in order to find yourself and your purpose, you have to dig deeper. Most people get so wrapped up in the maya of day-to-day life that unless you put forth effort and inner discernment, your purpose and the fulfillment that comes with it can be overlooked in the humdrum of normalcy. The daily expectations life brings can take up all of your time if you let them. They will chip away at your inner prosperity if daily life doesn't contain purpose and meaning. This is why work-life harmony (the W in The WELL Method) is a foundational concept. If you can make your career a part of your purpose in some way, you'll be compelled to dig deep each day and get familiar with what makes you unique, fulfilled, and happy. You'll continue to grow and evolve into a fulfilled being living a purpose-driven life.

Another thing that people mistake as purpose is excelling in their endeavors. Being successful or good at something doesn't necessarily mean it's your purpose. Exceptionally intelligent people often have the most difficulty finding and living their purpose because many things come easily to them. Remember that the E in The WELL Method stands for expect excellence. This is something we as humans need to do in every endeavor we undertake. It's part of a solid foundation of living; in and of itself, it is not purpose but a way to cultivate fulfillment through living your purpose. We've been trained to see high intelligence as a gift, and while it can undoubtedly be one, it can also be a hinderance to happiness. This is a great example of perspective and seeing how something can be used to make us happy or make us miserable. Even something that most everyone would perceive as good can be a detriment if not used wisely. Hence, this is why I'm a huge advocate for ditching labels and reevaluating societal norms and perceptions. Evaluating something on your own allows an unbiased look at the positive and negative in a situation so you can make the most out of it.

Create Your Purpose Plan

Now that you know what creates your purpose and may even have an idea of what it is, it's time to dive in and create your personalized Purpose Plan. We're going to look at everything that makes you unique and whole and set up a blueprint to fill in as you continue with this book. Knowing your purpose is only half of the picture; the next part is cultivating daily habits that will support it, and that is the focus of Part II in this book.

Step #1: Write down your innate talents that are conferred by your elemental type. If you did this before, kudos! If not, it's time to do it now. Write your answers below.

Figure 4-2: your innate talents. This can overlap with some of the things you wrote in Figure 4-1 but should also include specific things & not just attributes of your personality.

1.	6.
2.	7.
3.	8.
4.	9.
5.	10.

Step #2: Write down the things you enjoy or the ones you are interested in trying.

Figure 4-3: things I want to try & things I feel drawn to.

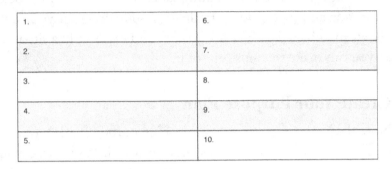

1.	6.
2.	7.
3.	8.
4.	9.
5.	10.

Step #3: Write down your most impactful life experiences. Maybe you only have one major thing and that is fine. Think of up to three things that have majorly impacted your life and have shaped who you've become. (Figure 4-4)

Step #4: Write down three things you believe your purpose could be that combines something from all three previous sections (innate talents, interests, and the emotions left by your personal experiences). Here's an example:

I find purpose by inspiring others through my writings. Writing is a conduit for me to guide others towards health and well-being.

Figure 4-5: ideas of what my purpose is.

1.
2.
3.

Figure 4-4: my most impactful life experiences.

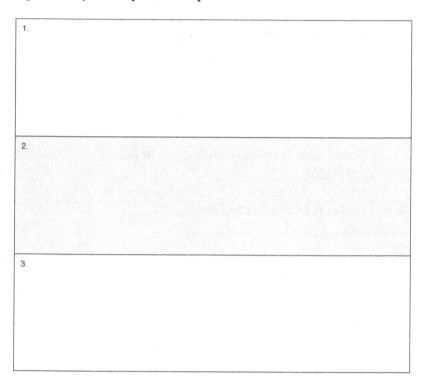

Step #5: Write down some ideas of what this might look like for you. Make sure it's something you can actually envision yourself doing and not just a hypothetical possibility. If you are unable to connect with it, don't write it down. If you feel it, this could be a conduit of expression for your purpose.

Let's use the example above: I find purpose by inspiring others through my writings. Writing is a conduit for me to guide others towards health and well-being. Here's what this might look like in this example:

1.
2.
3.

Now, use your answers from Step #4 to fill this in with ideas you can explore.

Figure 4-6: what my purpose may look like.

1.
2.
3.
4.
5.
6.

Leave this next section blank until you read through Part II of this book. Once you've completed it, come back and fill in this table, as it will be your guidepost for how to accomplish your purpose in day-to-day life.

Figure 4-7: my Purpose Plan & blueprint for a purpose-filled, healthy life.

My Purpose Plan	Idea #1	Idea #2
Breathwork Practice		
Daily Mindfulness		
Daily Meditation		
My Primary Elemental Type		
Facing Fear of Change		
Food for Mood		
My Exercise		
My Personal Affirmation		
Sacred Space		

Daily Steps to Live Your Purpose

The people who are most successful and happy are the ones who figure out a way to live their purpose each and every day. This builds inner prosperity and self-worth. Maintaining purpose is easy, but cultivating it to begin with takes effort, as we will discuss in the next section of this book. You'll learn exactly how things like affirmation, meditation, mindfulness, diet, and exercise play a role in cultivating a fulfilled and purpose-driven lifestyle and how these things also play a major role in your physical health and well-being. For now, let's look at three key things you can do to start cultivating healthy habits in day-to-day life.

Tip #1—Daily "Me Time"

The number one most important thing you can do for yourself is to create a daily habit of doing something just for you that you really enjoy. We will get more into consistency and how it impacts the mind in the chapter on mindfulness, but long before you start to cultivate a mindfulness practice, pick one consistent thing to do for yourself each and every day that makes you happy. You want to know why people make New Year's resolutions and then don't stick with them? It's simple, actually. It's because most people set resolutions for things they want to change in their lives, which involves work and effort, and yet, these people don't even have a daily practice of doing something meaningful to promote their own happiness. If you can't make the time and space necessary to nourish your soul, you'll surely not be able to make time or space when it requires actual work to accomplish your goal. This is the exact same reason many people don't stay consistent with a mindfulness practice.

In order to embrace the aspects of life that take work, you must first have the inner fuel necessary, and you cultivate this through the little things done each day that promote joy. Small daily habits that make you happy build strong neural connections in the brain that will help keep you happy. Whenever someone comes to me to learn a meditation practice, I always start them with a daily self-care routine. Otherwise, my experience has shown that psychologically and emotionally, the person will not be able to sustain it in the long run.

By doing something that makes you happy, you'll have the extra energy and motivation needed to do the more difficult work of making change and beginning practices that help you to expect excellence from yourself.

Tip #2—Wake Up Before Sunrise

Yogic and spiritual teachings believe there is a correlation between when you wake up and how your day will progress. By waking up before sunrise and being fully awake to greet the rising sun, you'll find that you have more focus, confidence, willpower, and motivation during your day, and you'll likely be able to accomplish more. It's a basic biological instinct to see sunrise as the start of the day and sunset as the end of it, so when you wake up late, it can leave you feeling like you've already missed out or are somehow running behind, trying to play catch up. When you wake up early, this lends itself to a feeling of being able to accomplish all of your goals for the day.

I suggest keeping a journal for two weeks where you write down how you're feeling, your motivation levels, and what you get done, and correlate this to when you wake up. When you wake up, make sure to set a plan for your day and have a good idea of all you want to accomplish. Just this simple habit of when you wake up can make a world of difference in your mental and emotional state.

Tip #3—Make Time for Introspection

I consider introspection to be a part of mindfulness, but since mindfulness is such a broad topic, I want to speak specifically about introspection and inner discernment here. Creating your WELL Method blueprint and Purpose Plan can help you reach all of your goals in life but only when you take the time to look at where you've come from and evaluate where you're going. Introspection requires you to be fully open and honest with yourself about your successes and shortcomings. When you can learn to do this in a neutral, non-judgmental way, the door to your highest potential opens up. Life ebbs and flows with both success and failure, so take both in stride. Look at the effort you've put into your life and evaluate how it's helped you live your purpose and cultivate a healthy life.

You may not see the entire forest because of the trees in front of you, but having daily time to introspect will allow you a bigger view of the forest over time. You'll be able to see things and understand how behaviors and habits correlate to outcomes in your life. Introspection is the best way to eliminate your personal blind spots—those parts that are so unconscious you don't even see them. By shedding more light and more attention onto what you can see, you'll start to uncover those things you can't see clearly, until they become clear as crystal.

Introspection, by its definition, requires you to be honest and neutral about what you find in yourself. It's a state of witnessing your own story, and through witnessing it, you can more clearly see what's working and what's not. If you find it difficult to be neutral in your perspective, take a step back and outside of yourself. Pretend you are watching a story of someone else's life and afford this story the same compassion you would another human being. This is part of the power behind witnessing your life and the lives of others; it connects you to empathy and compassion of the human experience so you can be gentler with yourself and use your findings to gently nudge yourself in the right direction.

Give these three things a try, and you'll see how they help you with everything you'll be learning in Part II of this book.

PART II

THE PATH FROM PURPOSE TO WELLNESS

My life reached a point where I was at a standstill. After being diagnosed with fibromyalgia, I lost my job, and my home was foreclosed on because I couldn't pay my mortgage. I was at literal rock bottom with no money, no roof over my head, and no seeming way forward since conventional Western medicine was ineffective in helping me recover. I had a decision to make: stay sick and permanently disabled from fibromyalgia or find a way to be well and thrive. Making a choice was step one in my journey towards purpose, and I chose to be well and thrive.

Interestingly, this is not just my story, but also that of world-renowned fibromyalgia expert Dr. Teitelbaum, creator of the SHINE Protocol. Here is what he told me about his experience: "Fibromyalgia, after a nasty viral illness, knocked me out of medical school and left me homeless for a year. Having been totally failed by the medical profession, I found recovery using a holistic approach. Our published research shows that people with fibromyalgia improve dramatically (90 percent on average) using the SHINE Protocol. This integrates Sleep, Hormones, Immunity, Nutrition, and Exercise as able. Adding the mind-body component of learning to say 'NO' to things that feel bad is another critical piece. Otherwise, people with fibromyalgia find themselves being dinner for every energy vampire in town!"

If Dr. Teitelbaum's approach was known to me when I was suffering, it would have inspired me to push forward with more confidence. Getting healthy was my priority, but since I didn't know how to do that at the time, I chose to focus on something I could control—my life's purpose and finding mental and emotional well-being. My life needed a major realignment. Little did I know at that time, the journey I would take towards changing my life and realigning with my true purpose was the exact same journey that would cause me to get well and be healthier than I'd ever been.

You see, it's not the major things we do that lead to the most lasting change but the small things we do each day that lead to moving mountains. In Part I, you gained conceptual clarity of the cornerstones of well-being; in Part II, you'll learn the small and simple things to do daily that'll enable you to accomplish the goals you set. The next few chapters outline the practical steps I took to align with my purpose and my health, in the order that I implemented these changes in my life. Order is everything. If you try to run before walking, you will fail. Likewise, if you try to reach your destination without walking the path to get there, where will you end up?

The steps we take on our journey are just as important as the destination itself—perhaps even more so. It's the steps that make you whole and complete, not the destination itself. The steps bring perspective, gratitude, and compassion to the journey we call life, which in turn influence our thoughts, behaviors, and actions towards others. While I hope you never have to go through everything I did, it made me who I am, and I have no regrets. Just know that no matter where you are in your journey or what you are dealing with, you can accomplish great things and turn your life around for the better. Now let's get started.

CHAPTER 5

JUST BREATHE

The very beginning of your journey, whether you're pursuing a life of purpose or a life of good health, starts with how you breathe. The breath holds a tremendous amount of life force, also known as *prana* or *chi*. In fact, we get more life force from our breath than from the food we eat! That's pretty crazy since we think of food as being the primary way of getting nourishment and energy, when in fact, most of it comes from how we utilize our breath. Does this mean if you learn to work with your breath that you'll need less food? It may indeed, especially if breathwork is combined with movement like walking, exercise, or yoga.

The breath is an abundant source of life force that can be used to optimize physical, mental, and emotional well-being. Intentional breathing brings focus and attention to the body and mind, making it easier to connect this potent form of prana to healing both the body and mind. Since breathing is usually an unconscious thing, people miss out on its true power and potent healing abilities. Whatever you bring your attention to, combined with life-force energy, you can start to heal or even just facilitate change or growth in. When you give your undivided attention to something, you bear witness to it. This act of bearing witness and giving someone or something your undivided attention is enough in and of itself to start making change. Just the act of bringing your attention to areas of pain or discomfort in the body is enough to start dissipating the pain or discomfort. Think of the importance of Lamaze during childbirth. While it won't get rid of all the pain, it does help to make the pain more bearable!

This may seem like a miracle or a placebo effect, but it's not. More than 70 percent of what goes on in and around you has become either subconscious or unconscious, meaning that it's happening with no effort on your part. Breathwork practices bring intention to an area, making it conscious again. And this small change of giving something energy, versus it not having your energy or focus, is what starts the cycle of healing. Breath and mindfulness go hand in hand, as you'll see here and the next chapter.

Breathing & the Mind

Let's first look at how breath is connected to the mind, because the breath and mindfulness connection sets the stage for better mental health and also emotional and physical well-being. The breath is directly connected to how your mind functions. If you want to learn to control your mind, it can be as simple as learning to control and master your breathing. Slow your breathing, and you'll dissipate the turbulence and scattered nature that accompanies your thoughts. Lengthening and deepening the breath, in and of itself, will cause the mind to calm down and focus better and can lead to less stress, less anxiety, and less mental turmoil. Less mental turmoil means less emotional stress. A calmer mind leads to a clearer, more focused mind and a positive emotional state. This has been so well researched that even Harvard University has information available via their website discussing the connection between relaxation, well-being, and breathwork.

Many people have adopted unhelpful breathing patterns which have a corresponding negative effect on mood and mindset. This may include shallow breathing, only breathing into part of the body (such as the shoulders), or holding the breath when fear strikes. Fun fact: did you know that fear cannot exist when you breathe through it? Part of the reason fear paralyzes people is because they stop breathing. Think about how you react when you get frightened. The body's normal response is to freeze when you hold your breath unless you put forth conscious effort to change this. Because we stop breathing temporarily when fear strikes, the fearful emotion you're experiencing gets locked in the mind. Once you consciously start breathing again, deeply and into all parts of the body, fear subsides, and the mind will come back to center. Remember this next time something scares you, as it'll enable you to calm down quickly.

Fear is the most prominent example of how breathing affects people, but how you breathe corresponds to practically every emotion people experience and will have a direct impact on mood. The typical shallow breathing patterns people adopt cause the body to be tense and rigid, which causes rigidity in one's mindset and emotions. Conversely, breathing deep into your belly and focusing the breath all throughout the body leads to deeper relaxation and a general sense of well-being.

So why do people breathe shallow to begin with? One reason comes down to body image. Men and women are both taught a cultural narrative that your belly should be toned and slender.

This act of body shaming leads to shallow chest breathing, which affects not just overall energy levels and ability to move prana in the body, but also affects mood, mindset, and mental acuity. This pattern becomes habitual and unconscious, and we forget we're even doing it. I'll discuss habits and how to form new ones more in depth in the next chapter on mindfulness.

If you want to learn different ways to use the breath to facilitate mental clarity, physical well-being, and positive emotions, look no further than yoga. While yoga itself relies on an eight-limbed path originating from Patanjali's Yoga Sutras, yoga asana (the physical exercise) teaches a lot about breathwork and how breath affects a person's overall well-being. Yogic philosophy believes that the more you slow your breath, the better health you'll be in. It also teaches how to pair different breathing patterns to activate heating or cooling energies in the body and, when in combination with yoga poses, can move prana throughout the body. In essence, you can target the breath to work on just about any area of the body to improve health and well-being, improve digestion, cleanse the emotions, clear the mind, and gain more energy. The beauty of yoga is that while it originates as an Eastern philosophy, it doesn't matter what your belief system or religion is. Anyone can practice the physical and mindfulness aspects of yoga to benefit their lives without being in conflict with their beliefs.

Breath-Per-Minute Analysis

One of the things I've learned through my study of yoga and Eastern traditions is that there is a general breath rate that corresponds to good health and overall well-being. Here's an exercise for you to determine how many complete breaths you take in the course of a single minute.

1. Sit down comfortably and set a timer for one minute.

2. Take your first inhalation once you start the timer: an inhalation and exhalation are considered one complete breath.

3. Continue until your timer stops at one minute. Count how many complete breaths you have taken (keep track as you do the exercise).

Some yoga traditions teach that the average human takes about fifteen breaths per minute. If your breath-per-minute rate is higher, you're likely heading towards poor health. When your breath per minute rate drops below fifteen, your body is able to regenerate and heal itself more quickly and even prevent illness in the first place. Strive to get your resting breath rate to fifteen or less. It's normal that your breathing rate will be slower while you do this exercise for the simple reason that you are bringing attention to your breath. That's perfectly normal. Just do your best to breathe normally and not alter your normal breathing patterns so that your assessment is as accurate as possible.

Since the mind and breath are directly connected, adept meditators are known to drastically slow their breath rate during the practice of meditation. Yogic philosophy teaches that people who can slow their breath down to four breaths per minute will activate their pituitary gland located at the third eye, while those who can slow it down to one a minute can activate the pineal gland connected to the crown chakra. Don't try this at home, as it definitely won't come naturally! Working with the breath is something that with just a small amount of practice will come naturally, and that is when you start seeing its benefits in day-to-day life.

Working with my breath and becoming conscious of it was one of the first things I did on my journey to rebuild my life. By working with it consistently and daily, I was able to retrain my resting breath to a normal breath-per-minute rate of seven to eight. In day-to-day life, this translates to a lot of good things. I rarely get sick anymore. I can't even remember the last time I went to a doctor for anything illness related. Even before I was diagnosed with fibromyalgia, I would get sick frequently—at least once every few weeks. That all stopped within a few months of slowing my breathing. Altering my normal breathing pattern also had a profound impact on my mind and the way I perceive the world in that I react much less and find myself consciously responding to what life brings. This is a natural effect when the mind is less cluttered and turbulent.

Practical Tips for Day-to-Day Life

You don't need to become a yogi to use breathing to your benefit. You already know that lengthening and slowing the breath can have a profound impact on your mood, health, and mindset, and that the mere act of witnessing your breath can start the cycle of change. Making lasting changes in your life is as simple as taking five minutes a day to sit and practice deepening your breath. The average person spends an hour a day on social media, so I'm sure you can carve out five minutes to work on your breath.

Don't forget about the profound spiritual connections between breath and life. Life force is power, and some people see life force energy as a manifestation of God. Your breath is a direct connection between you and your higher power. It's a constant reminder that you are enough, and there is always enough energy at your disposal to change and heal your life. Since all forms of life force are a part of God, it's a way to remember that you are never alone. You are always supported and nourished. Sometimes we just need a reminder of this. You can use your breathwork practice as a means of remembering and honoring God in day-to-day life.

Practice breathing into all parts of the body. Bring your attention to different body parts while you sit and breathe deeply. Try breathing all the way down into your feet. How does this feel different from your normal breath? Breathe deep into your belly, then let the breath fill your lungs, chest, and shoulders. Next, work to fully exhale the breath from all of these areas. After you do this exercise a couple of times, it should be easy to figure out how you normally breathe and what you can work on specifically. I used to breathe primarily into my chest, and I found that my breath was very shallow most of the time. After repeated practice, my new norm is breathing deeply into the abdomen, then expanding into the chest. Whatever becomes your new norm will be what becomes comfortable for you. The key to making these small changes lead to profound results is to let the new behavior become your norm so that new neural connections are made in the brain. Then you won't even have to think about your breath or put effort into it. This new healthy pattern will happen on its own, allowing you to take the next step forward on your path to purpose and well-being.

Breath & The WELL Method

Breathwork is directly connected to the E (expect excellence) and final L (love, not fear) of The WELL Method. Part of expecting excellence is in cultivating daily habits that help you keep your mind and emotions positive and clear. Be aware of what it takes to succeed, and do what you can each and every day to support it. Use your strengths and practical tips like breathwork to minimize weaknesses and expecting excellence will become second nature.

Breath is a simple yet very effective way to pave the road to purpose. As we discussed earlier, fear paralyzes the breath, so in order to get unstuck and come back to a place of making good decisions, you have to breathe. Having a daily breathwork practice can help retrain your mind to walk straight through fear so that it can't take control. Fear is just an illusion and not something you ever want to base decisions on. Love is its opposite: open, giving, and courageous. A small amount of breathwork, even two to three minutes a day, is enough to start changing your perspective and take power away from fear, stress, anxiety, depression, and self-doubt.

Using Breath to Deal with a Bad Day

We all have bad days from time to time. Negative emotions will impact the breath, just as breath impacts your emotions. It goes both ways. You can use the power of breathwork to change your emotions and come back to a place of well-being.

A simple and extremely effective practice for this is to regulate the inhalation and exhalation, combined with adding pauses after you've inhaled and after you've exhaled. This will take you less than three minutes:

1. Time your inhalation to measure four seconds, then hold your breath in for four seconds.

2. Time your exhalation to measure four seconds, then hold your breath out for four seconds.

3. Repeat eight to ten times.

By keeping all four parts equal lengths, you are effectively resetting your mind to come back to a state of harmony. Once you've practiced this a few times, you can expand each step to five seconds, then six seconds, and so on as a way to practice lengthening and deepening your breathing. Make sure that you are always comfortable: there is no need to push yourself to a place of discomfort. Being comfortable will help instill the feelings of well-being you're looking to gain, even if you're only comfortable doing the technique at four second intervals. The length of each doesn't matter as long as each step is kept to the same length of time.

Use these breathwork practices each day, and you'll start to see a shift in your thoughts, emotions, and overall well-being. It'll set the stage for creating an effective mindfulness or meditation practice and minimize the effort you'll need to put into your practice. Mindfulness without understanding your breath is not sustainable for creating an effective practice. When you understand the power of breath first, most of the work of being mindful is already done. We'll discuss this more in the next chapter.

CHAPTER 6

WHAT'S GOING ON IN YOUR HEAD?

Working with mindfulness, meditation, and breathwork combined is where my life really started to shift in a profound way, and as you know, this is just the beginning of the journey. There was a new sense of possibility that opened up, like a breath of fresh air. I knew for the first time in a very long time there was hope. I used to suffer from both anxiety and depression (in addition to fibromyalgia), and the anxiety would get so bad sometimes that I had a prescription for Xanax. Within two months of daily mindfulness and meditation practice, I was witnessing profound changes to my mood and well-being. Within six months, I never had to take medication for anxiety ever again. Within a year, I stopped getting sick altogether; that's right—no more colds or bacterial infections. It took a bit longer to completely heal from fibro, but we'll get to that as we continue this journey. Without a doubt, I can say that meditation and mindfulness were my foundations to well-being. These are what everything else was, and is, built on.

So, what *is* going on in your head? Probably lots of things, all at the same time. There are things that are consciously in the front of your mind and things on the back burner that'll pop up when you're less busy. Then there's those crazy thoughts that have no context and appear out of nowhere, and even the very odd things that come to mind when you enter a dream state. Even if you have about ten things on your mind all at once, don't worry. You can retrain your mind to focus on things you want to think about while eliminating the scattered thoughts that make you distracted, tired, and unproductive.

The mind can be one of two things: a wastebasket that accumulates trash and becomes toxic to your environment, or the projector of your reality. If you don't take the trash out frequently, it starts to smell and become a burden. The same thing happens with all the things that accumulate in the mind. The waste needs to be eliminated before it starts causing problems to your health and well-being—not just mental, but physical too. Mind waste can be looked at as all of the different stimuli we encounter and process on a daily basis. Things the conscious, subconscious, and even unconscious mind are making decisions about whether you realize it or not. In a fraction of a second, your mind can assess a situation for safety, gauge how you feel about someone you've just met, and even let you know how to respond to what your coworker just said. The mind encounters thousands of stimuli each day, and how we process them all is the difference between being mentally unwell (even mentally ill), stressed, and in poor physical health, or being clear-headed, focused, relaxed, healthy, and able to create the life you want to live. In order to clear out mental waste and have your mind start working for you, you'll first need to understand how the mind functions and the differences between mindfulness and meditation. Let's dive in.

A Look at Mindfulness

Mindfulness is an act of bringing conscious awareness to a particular issue. It gives a focal point, which means you can make conscious change to an area of your life quickly. Mindfulness can be as simple as becoming aware of what is happening right here, right now. It's easy to get lost in your thoughts, feelings, or even stress and not realize those things are influencing your thoughts and actions. Learning to come back to the present moment and differentiate the here and now from what's happening in your mind is a great place to start a mindfulness practice. Being mindful reminds you that you are not the stress or thoughts you're dealing with. This simple shift in perspective enables you to redirect your mind towards things that create inner prosperity and positivity, while avoiding what doesn't. Let's learn a technique to do this, called the Five Sense Check-in.

Mindful Technique—The Five Sense Check-in

I love this technique because it's quick, highly effective, and simple to master. We talked about this in chapter 2. This technique does more than bring you into the now; it teaches you how to witness yourself and step outside of the mind. To do a Five Sense Check-in, you're literally going to tune into each of the five senses and note what you are experiencing right now. What do you smell? For example, maybe there is lingering odor for the food you recently ate. Maybe there are flowers nearby that have a nice fragrance. What do you taste? What do you see? Lastly, what physical sensations do you feel in your body, and what do you hear? Each sensory perception is connected to the mind and memory, and each offers an opportunity to be mindful.

Sit down and take a moment to tune into each of these and write down what you notice for each. Start with smell, then move to taste, then sight, then touch, then sound, respectively. It may take a bit of time to tune into some of these, and that's okay. Once you're able to tune into each one, you may not even remember what you were thinking about before you started the exercise! It's that powerful. You can use this sensory check-in technique any time you need to tune in and make sure you are present and not locked up in your mind.

Figure 6-1: write down what you notice after you complete the Five Sense Check-in.

Sense Perception	What do you notice?
Smell	
Taste	
Sight	
Touch/Feeling	
Sound/Hearing	

Mindfulness as Self-Inquiry

Once you're comfortable cultivating awareness of the present moment, you can take your mindfulness practice to the next level by delving into self-inquiry and using it as a way to analyze your reaction patterns and belief systems. Self-inquiry, also known as inner discernment, is the key to understand how your past has created your present and how your present actions will create your future. Using mindfulness to dissect and redirect thoughts is a powerful way to rewire the neural connections in your brain to form good habits that'll support the purpose-driven, healthy life you're creating. For example, let's look at Dan, who has a fear and strong dislike of dogs. Even the cute, fluffy little guys! Every time a dog comes into the office or Dan passes one on the street, he tenses up and gets angry.

Self-inquiry has enabled Dan to take a step back and look at this situation from an outsider's point of view. Many dogs are genuinely loving creatures; they're not called man's best friend for nothing! Dan knows this, and Dan knows the dog he met on the street today was not going to hurt him, yet he still got upset and fearful. Why? Well, Dan was bitten by a dog when he was a child, and that resulted in him needing stitches for the injury. Overall, it was a traumatic emotional experience for a young child. The thought form that experience created has stuck with Dan, and every time he sees a dog, it triggers it, resulting in a negative bias towards all dogs.

This is a great example of what it means to be present in the now and not in the past. Thought distortions, like Dan's dislike of dogs, will stick around until you heal them and rewire the neural connection in your brain. By being mindful, Dan can redirect his thoughts. The next time he encounters a friend's dog, Dan will tell himself this is not the dog that hurt him, and this dog deserves love. He will witness how his friend's dog is cute and loving and start to connect new emotions to his memory of dogs. Doing this repeatedly will retrain Dan's mind and diminish the painful childhood experience that created the thought form. Step one for Dan was being aware his reaction to all dogs was biased; step two is to put in conscious effort to push through this thought distortion and eliminate the thought form that created it.

What's your trigger? What people or situations trigger you to have an innate and inaccurate bias? One common example is a person's name. Say you had a loving brother named Marcus and a terrible bully at school named Doug. When you meet someone new named Marcus, you're likely to have an affinity, and a repulsion when it comes to meeting someone named Doug.

Dig into these patterns, because we all have them. It would be impossible to not be shaped and molded by our experiences and environment. It's a very normal part of life, and remember, experience is half of what helps us know our true purpose. We just need to become aware of how much bias is present and how it impacts our day-to-day lives. Any form of bias, like the examples given, is an indication that you are not in the present moment. What has happened in the past is not an indication of the present or future, but it becomes an almost certainty when you choose to react in the same way you did in the past. By taking note if your choices are conscious responses or subconscious reactions based on bias, you can use mindfulness to create the purpose-filled life you want.

Mindfulness is essential when figuring out what it means to be true to yourself. What do you believe and value? Is it the things you've been taught from others, or do you just believe those things because that's what you've been exposed to in your life? Using inner discernment as a mindfulness technique can help you to be honest with yourself about what you value by learning to understand where your beliefs came from. Once you know the origin, you can reevaluate the belief or action pattern and see if it fits with the purpose-driven life you're creating. Use it to reevaluate societal norms too, to see if they fit into your life.

Not everyone has to grow up, get married, have 2.5 kids, and have a house in the suburbs. If you realize some of the things you've been taught don't fit with your picture of happiness, then it's time to make some new beliefs, and we do this by forming new habits.

Anything that becomes a habit is something the mind will become comfortable with and begin to crave. Just because something has been your norm for a long time, maybe even a lifetime, doesn't mean it's right; it just means you've grown accustomed to it and normalized it. Most importantly, you can change it, no matter what "it" is. Did you learn bad eating habits as a child? Were you taught to worry about things instead of seeing the abundance in life? Maybe you grew up in a family of racists who looked down on people of other cultures or religions. Whatever it was for you, mindfulness is your most powerful weapon to create a new story for your life. Get out of your box. Experience what the world has to offer and try new things. Meet new people who you think are different than you. Trying new things helps the mind confront whatever it has made normal. New things may feel wrong at first, but this is just because they aren't normal to us. Given time and repeated exposure to new things, you can retrain the mind to adopt these new experiences wholeheartedly. Remember the final L in The WELL Method: love, not fear. Mindfulness is the key to it, because it takes effort to do things differently. It takes real courage to create your own story and choose what is a part of what makes you "you."

Now, let's talk about meditation because, combined with mindfulness, you can take charge of your thoughts, your beliefs, and your health.

A Look at Meditation

When I spoke to world-renowned author Dr. Susan Shumsky about meditation, her story was similar to my own. She also believes meditation is central for a successful, healthy life and has been practicing for over fifty years. Susan said, "It was 1967 when I first started meditating, and it healed my life. I believe that meditation is the panacea of all ills. It's like a miracle in anyone's life. It takes you to a place of centeredness of being and complete integration by bringing you into your true self. There are countless benefits of meditation, including better emotional stability, better mental health, and also better physical health. There's a lot of scientific research that's been done on meditation and, time and time again, it shows the benefits."

Dr. Josh Axe, DNM, CNS, DC, is also a powerful proponent of meditation, although you probably know him for his books and top website on health. Dr. Axe is the founder of Ancient Nutrition and DrAxe.com, the author of the best-selling books *Keto Diet* and *Collagen Diet*, and the host of The Dr. Axe Show. He says, "I believe that just about everybody, myself included, benefits from daily restorative practices like meditation—whether done in a traditional manner like sitting still in silence, or while exercising, walking, or doing yoga. Various types of meditation, as well as prayer, help me in a number of ways—including by improving how I deal with stress, giving me clarity, and allowing me to live in line with my values/purpose/intentions. These acts also help me to keep an open mind when trying to solve problems, take my attention off of myself so I can see another's viewpoint more clearly, and remind me that I'm not alone in any problem I'm dealing with."

Earlier, I defined mindfulness as an act of bringing conscious awareness to a particular issue. Meditation is a practice that uses silence and emptiness to heal the subconscious and unconscious minds, and also the physical body. Remember how I said earlier that the mind can either be a wastebasket accumulating garbage or be the projector of your reality? Meditation is how we empty the wastebasket. Here's my favorite analogy: The stomach and intestines digest the food we eat each day. Food is turned into energy, and the leftover waste products are eliminated, lest they build up and make us sick. Meditation is the digestion process of the mind. Meditation takes all of the stimuli we've reacted to during the course of a day and digests them, essentially dissolving them into non-existence. With these stimuli gone, the mind doesn't get scattered or cluttered. You're able to focus more easily and have ample energy for any task at hand. When those stimuli aren't digested, they build up and start to distort what's happening in the mind. It's like a haze that clouds over the mind and causes wires to get crossed and short-circuit.

Figure 6-2: the mind gets overwhelmed & bogged down by the external stimuli we encounter each day. Meditation digests it all, leaving the mind clear and running smoothly.

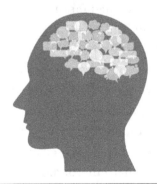

BEFORE   **AFTER**

Meditation's effectiveness at getting rid of these stimuli and background chatter reduces anxiety and stress and can even alleviate symptoms of depression. Meditation also improves the health of your physical body. There have been many scientific studies done that show how a daily meditation practice boosts immunity, improves heart heath, lowers blood pressure, reduces stress, helps balance hormones, improves sleep, and can even reduce cognitive decline associated with aging. And these are just a few examples of what has been backed up by science. Meditation can essentially help with every area of life: from health to work to relationships to personal development. There's nothing a daily meditation practice can't make better.

We know meditation gets rid of waste accumulated in the mind. It also helps to digest and process emotional connections we have to experiences. When powerful emotions latch on to an experience, thought forms are created that give memories a life of their own. Thought forms cause a distortion and bias in our action and reaction patterns, like Dan's dislike of dogs. The emotion was so strong that it created a thought form that impacted Dan long after a dog bit him.

When thought forms are from bad experiences, it can feel like you're reliving trauma over and over again, or like a cloud is looming over you that you just can't seem to get rid of (think of how PTSD affects people). For less traumatic experiences, it can be like a nagging persistent negativity or self-doubt that sticks with you. Thought forms created from negative experiences are nearly synonymous with what Eckhart Tolle refers to as the "pain body," although thought forms can also take on positive emotional manifestations that propel us forward. Positive thought forms help build inner prosperity, whereas the negative ones can dip people into a place of inner poverty.

Meditation is the most powerful tool a person has at their disposal to deal with accumulated thought forms. It's the way you heal your past and make room in the present, mentally and emotionally, to build the life you want. Meditation is like peeling an onion: it peels away the outer layers first then works its way inward, dealing with what is most pressing at the moment before working its way inward to deeper levels of awareness.

Think of a traumatic experience you've faced (nearly all people have in one way or another). That experience has created a series of reaction patterns, stored emotions, thought forms, and many subtle things that affect day-to-day life. They can be so subtle that you don't even recognize them. The patterns that we've put in place are like the outer layers of the onion. They have to be eliminated before you can get to the source of the issue. It's like the trash pile that gets bigger and bigger. Until you remove what's on top and throw it away, you can't get to the stuff that has been there the longest. The great thing about meditation is that it knows how to perfectly unwind and digest these experiences in a way that brings you back to a place where you'll no longer have emotional pain or trauma. The memory will be there, but it will be devoid of any form of emotional connection, and this is how you know you've healed the issue.

The magic of meditation is that it unbundles stimuli and emotions from the conscious, subconscious, and unconscious minds in a way that enables you to grow and change with no conscious effort at all on your part. Mindfulness brings conscious attention to an issue, so when combined it's like adding a turbo-booster to your fuel.

Elemental Types, Mindfulness & Meditation

Each element is connected to a sensory perception. If your constitution is strong in a particular element, you'll likely find it easy to tune into that sense. Let's say you're strong in the fire element; you're probably hyper tuned into what you see, and less so on the elements that are not as strong a part of your constitution. I have practically no air element in my constitution, so for me, the sense of touch is not nearly as important as is sound or smell. That means if I don't put conscious effort towards it, I'll probably not notice what I'm feeling in my body. It enables me to push past pain, but it also means I can push myself too far without noticing it. Presence requires us to tune into and be aware of all our sense perceptions, lest we slip out of mindfulness and into reaction patterns.

When it comes to meditation and certain mindfulness techniques, you can use elements you're strong in as a focal point to calm the mind. Meditation techniques employ focus usually on a mantra (sound), an image (sight), or the breath (touch), which is no coincidence as our sense perceptions are so strong. Use ones that play to your elemental strengths, and you'll resonate better with it and find your practice much more effective. In fact, I've found this to be key to cultivating a lasting, successful meditation practice.

Meditation techniques often use sensory perception as a focal point for the mind. You can use a meditation technique to more quickly reach a place of silent meditation because it helps the mind to center and calm down. Meditation techniques are different than silent meditation, in that techniques train the mind to focus on one particular thing to the exclusion of everything else. This is active and conscious. Silent meditation is the exact opposite; you let your mind slip away into nothingness, letting thoughts pass you by. Merely for the sake of definitions, I would classify a meditation technique as a form of mindfulness because it's taking conscious effort and meditation as what happens when you go into the silence with no effort or thought involved.

Any technique that is conscious and active can be used to train the mind, hone your skills, and cultivate excellence in yourself (the E in The WELL Method). You can use techniques to focus on just about anything, including creating positivity, cultivating gratitude, or even strengthening memory and cognitive function. Silent meditation, though, is the key to well-being. It's what heals the body and mind, and for that reason, it cannot be overlooked. The longer you sit in quiet and stillness, the more the body will be able to rejuvenate itself.

For a complete selection of meditation techniques paired to your unique elemental type, see my book *Vibrational Healing: Attain Balance & Wholeness. Understand Your Energetic Type.*

CHAPTER 7

WORK WITH YOUR UNIQUE ENERGY TYPE

You learned about elemental types in the very first chapter, so you have a good idea now about how they give rise to uniqueness in your personality, your body type and shape, and your unique gifts in life. You also know that it is your life's purpose that gives rise to your unique elemental type so that you are perfectly supported in fulfilling your purpose and being happy in life. So how can we work with our uniqueness in day-to-day life that makes a lasting impact? Let's dive into that now.

Both Ayurveda and traditional Chinese medicine have the fundamental understanding that different elemental types need different things to be successful—in terms of just about everything. This includes diet, types and times of exercise, remedies to common ailments, how you settle into sleep and how much you'll need, and even the specific well-being practices you adapt to keep mind, body, and soul in harmony. Being healing systems, they put a lot of emphasis on working with the body. We're going to take this a step further and learn how to work with your unique type specifically to promote mental and emotional well-being and inner prosperity, and to work with your personal WELL Method goals.

What Works for You?

When I started meditating and being mindful, I also started looking at natural healing modalities that could help me get better quickly. I found a lot of garbage in it, even in the subjects of mindfulness and meditation. Garbage may be too harsh of a word; let's at least say it was garbage for me. Why is it that a particular meditation practice or healing modality gave me the heebie-jeebies or zapped my energy whereas others felt like a gift from God? It took me a long time to figure out (and I only did in retrospect and after lots of trial and error) that it came down to what was compatible with my elemental type. No technique or healing approach is inherently better than another, but you will find that some work better or worse for you.

This is an important concept for many reasons on an individual and societal level. It emphasizes why it's important to understand how your elemental type and your personality affect you. It shows that fad trends and one-size-fits-all approaches don't work for everyone and that you have to find what works for you. Working with your unique type will make you grow a thick skin and develop confidence in yourself because it's not about what others think is best; it's literally about you knowing what is best for you. It's also about being wise enough to not assume what works for you will work for someone else.

It can be super discouraging to try the most recent "it" thing that has worked for thousands of people, only to find it doesn't work for you. For some people, that can be enough to dissuade them from trying again to find something that will work. Why didn't it work? I must be flawed, right (see the mind games we play when something doesn't work out)? No way, not in a million years. Get that thought distortion out of your head right now. It's likely because the "it" thing didn't fit your elemental type and, thus, didn't play to your strengths.

The danger in trying to stick with something that doesn't work for you or make you feel good about yourself, just because others say it works for them, is that it damages inner prosperity by undermining confidence in yourself. You're essentially telling yourself that your direct experience is less important than the opinions of others. It also damages your connection with God and the ability to have faith because, in feeling inadequate about yourself, your thoughts and feelings are communicating to yourself and the universe that God has not made you properly. Obviously, those words aren't coming out of your mouth, but they may as well be because it's the same thing. You have been perfectly made to fulfill your purpose and live a happy, healthy life. God doesn't make mistakes.

When inner prosperity is damaged, it's nearly impossible to pursue your sense of purpose, and it becomes more difficult to stay well physically, mentally, and emotionally. Stress and anxiety creep in along with self-doubt and diminished confidence. Getting back on track means saying no to what's not working for you. Now that you know it's likely due to your elemental type, you can focus on finding something that will work and ditch the blame game the mind likes to play.

The Spiritual Growth of Working with Your Type

Learning to work with my unique type was probably the longest part of my journey. It overlapped with later stages, but really solidifying this concept went beyond following my inner guidance and required me to become more confident and grow a thicker skin. It had spiritual implications as well that helped me evolve into a more tolerant, compassionate human being.

When I started meditating, I would go to a particular group meditation each week, and truth be told, I hated it. To this day I despise that technique. I didn't stick with it more than a few months, and it tainted my perception of the group that was using it. They thought the technique was great and treated me less than because I had a different opinion. Less than, as in less spiritually evolved and less likely to succeed—like I didn't belong. My difference in opinion made me an outsider. Being treated like I was not worthy or somehow flawed soured my perception even more, and I still can't think about that technique without remembering the spiritual egoism that group held on to and how their misguided beliefs made me feel.

Learning to be compassionate towards others and understanding that my right is not your right—that we all need different things to succeed—really is a process of spiritual growth. Spiritual ego creeps in when you think your way is the right or best way to do something. This is actually a global problem that's been around since probably the dawn of time. It's this same mentality that leads to religious wars, racism, prejudice, nationalism, classism, body shaming, and all of the other toxic thought distortions that divide humanity instead of uniting it. It's our differences that unite us, not divide us. Differences lead to synergies and help cultivate appreciation and beauty in life. This is why the final L in The WELL Method is "love, not fear." We are all unique individuals, and we will also always have things that unite us with others. Don't ever let your uniqueness be something that divides you or makes you think you're better (or less) than someone else. If someone else takes offense with you honoring your own needs, that's on them, but never be the one to instigate division because of differences. That ignites inner poverty and scarcity consciousness, and you need inner prosperity to fulfill your purpose.

None of us are islands. We all need mentoring and guidance from others in order to reach our goals. If you push away everyone who is not like you, how will you ever grow or learn the things you don't already know? Who will be there to challenge you or inspire you to greater heights? Who will show you a different point of view? Three of the four WELL Method cornerstones (all but W) have one thing in common that will help you succeed: cultivate as much diversity in your social sphere as possible. Accepting the diversity and differences in others will help you to fully accept yourself, and all the strengths and weaknesses that go along with being the perfectly, divinely created masterpiece that you are.

Elemental Type vs. Imbalances in Your Type

Whew! We've gotten through the tough part of type-based character development (a.k.a. eliminating spiritual egoism). Now let's look at how to identify your type vs. an imbalance in it.

Let's do a simple exercise here to help you hone in on your primary elemental types. Step one: using the figure below, what are two strongest senses? Circle them both. Step two: what's your body shape? Be honest here and circle the body shape category that best suits you. You'll probably have one element that you've circled in both the sensory perception and body shape categories. This is likely your primary element. The second sense perception you circled corresponds with what's likely your secondary element.

If you don't have an element with both circled, or just want to dive deeper, reference Figure 1-2 in this book for more corresponding attributes to help determine your primary and secondary elemental types. If you're still uncertain, then definitely get my book *Vibrational Healing: Attain Balance & Wholeness. Understand Your Energetic Type* for a complete breakdown and quizzes to determine your exact composition.

Figure 7-1: elements & their corresponding sensory perception & body shape.

Element	Sensory Perception	Body Shape
Earth	Smell	Gains weight easily, maybe curvy but not rounded body shape.
Water	Taste	Gains weight very easily, curvy in nature, rounded features especially in face.
Fire	Sight	Lose weight easily when effort is put in, otherwise stable.
Air	Touch/Feeling	Hard to gain weight, tall and slender build.
Space/Ether	Sound	Doesn't directly correlate to body shape.

Now, write down your primary and secondary elemental types:

Primary Element: _____
Secondary Element: _____

It's all too common for people to think something about their lifestyle or daily habits is due to their type when it's really due to an imbalance. Let's use food cravings as an example of this. People with predominant fire and air elements, the ones who tend towards being very slender with no effort, often stay away from heavier foods like potatoes, pastas, and the like, favoring lighter foods like salad and fresh fruits. That's actually an imbalance and not type-based!

We talked about embracing differences earlier. Well, this goes far beyond ethos and ideology. It's rooted in Ayurveda and TCM for taking care of the body too. Air and fire types should eat a good balance of heavier, calorically dense foods like pasta and potatoes because it's a perfect counterbalance to their light and airy nature. Conversely, people with lots of earth and water elements should have a good balance of lighter foods, limiting the heavier ones, to bring balance to their grounded, stable nature. If you know your constitution is primarily earth or water, and you find that you're always craving heavy foods, or if you're fire, air, or space elements and only want light foods like salad, that's a clear sign of an imbalance.

Having any sort of strong cravings is almost always a signal of imbalance yet is the number one thing people look to as evidence of their type. Since it can be counterintuitive, here are some telltale ways to know the difference.

Figure 7-2: signs of an imbalance in your elemental constitution.

What's Affected	Balanced Constitution	Signs of an Imbalance
Physical	Preferences that aren't as strong as cravings.	Cravings or repulsions.
Physical	Sustained mental and physical energy throughout the day.	Tiredness, fatigue, or low energy.
Mental	Hopeful and full of optimism.	Self-doubt or self-deprecation.
Mental	Mindful and present.	Thought distortions and thought forms.
Emotional	Inner calm or joy from seemingly nothing.	Increase in stress, anxiety, anger, or fear.
Emotional	Sustained good mood with no catalyst.	Urges, impulsive actions, or negative emotions.
Spiritual	Feeling included and loved.	Feeling unsupported or alone.
Spiritual	Strengths amplified with no effort.	Weaknesses are amplified.

If something is really a sign of your elemental type, it's going to harmonize and synergize all the parts of your being so that multiple things work together seamlessly. When synergy happens, two things act as one, amplifying the effects to something greater than the sum of its parts. Conversely, when imbalances arise, a particular thing takes more of your attention, diminishing the synergy of body and mind working together. This can be experienced as cravings or repulsions, or even a change in your thought patterns or emotions to reflect stronger than normal biases or feelings. Imbalances can also show up as thought distortions and may trigger latent thought forms to rear their ugly heads.

The key to keeping mind, body, and soul healthy is to rectify an imbalance when you first notice it. The longer it persists, the more your thoughts, emotions, and body will be affected, making the imbalance more difficult to resolve. If you know you're stressed out, take a break. Take some time to yourself for some self-care. If you're craving the wrong sorts of foods, make sure you're getting the right balance for you and not falling into bad patterns (you'll love the chapter on food for mood). A small bit of mindfulness applied to mind-body-soul harmony will go a long way towards building sustainable habits that help you succeed.

Not only can you identify an imbalance, you can tell when things are harmonized and working well for you because even your non-primary elements will start working in your favor. All of your senses become amplified in a positive way when synergy happens. For example, the air element is by far the weakest in my constitution, but when everything else is harmonized, I notice the very tangible benefits of the air element. There is a natural lightness; I sleep much less and have a ton of energy, and I innately want less food. My creativity is unlocked, and my thoughts become expansive and uplifted. Tastes are heightened; the sense of touch is more prominent. Smells may affect you more than normal. It's like the beauty in all things is amplified because you have the ability to experience everything through the senses more powerfully. Synergy is a win-win that enables you to experience everything in a more profound, meaningful way.

Use Strengths to Minimize Weaknesses in Your WELL Method and Purpose Plan

Your elemental type is the key to creating your personal WELL Method and Purpose Plan. Now that you know your two strongest elements, you're going to use the sensory perceptions that correlate to them as you create your plan. Since they are a fundamental part of you, as are the innate talents and gifts that also correspond to your elemental type, working with both daily will, in and of itself, help build inner prosperity and self-confidence. This is a powerful way of using your strengths to minimize your weaknesses. Simply put, do what you're good at and what you enjoy.

For example, if one of your strong elements is fire, you can pick a meditation for your routine that includes a visual element to help calm the mind. Maybe you'll use something in your home decor that has a strong visual component. Try adding spicy foods as part of your routine (spice is connected to the fire element). If your strong element is water, maybe you'll want to explore a mindful eating practice or new ways to incorporate new spices and flavors into your cooking. Take a long, hot bath at the end of the day. The more you engage your senses in a positive way, the more they will work to support you, becoming allies on your path. A key to spiritual connection is unity of mind, body, and soul, which is only possible when your five sense perceptions work in your favor.

Here are some attributes and strengths connected to the five elemental types that you may not realize. When creating your personalized plan, use self-inquiry to understand how these attributes affect your life, and where you can use your strengths to amplify inner prosperity and excellence in yourself. You can also refer back to Figure 1-2 for more elemental info.

Figure 7-3: elements, their attributes & some of their corresponding strengths.

Element	Attributes	Associated Strengths
Earth	Solid, rigid, fixed, dense.	Organized, methodical, grounded, leadership skills, writing skills, nurturing, teaching, consistent, precision-oriented, follow-through, makes ideas a tangible reality, healing energy.
Water	Fluid, takes the shape of its container.	Caring, compassionate, empathetic, nurturing, good listening skills, patience.
Fire	Spicy, destructive, hot.	Discerning, charismatic, leadership skills, no bs, direct, strong, clarity of thought, confidence, strong will, problem solving skills.
Air	Light and expansive.	Creative, ideas person, bubbly, energetic.
Space	Substance that holds the structure of each other element. Makes time linear.	Affinity for music, healing, design, use of patterns, shapes and colors, artistic, passionate, expansive, holds space for others.

Take a moment to remember how powerfully connected your thoughts, feelings, and experiences are to your health and well-being. Even a single day of negative emotions can cause enough stress to deplete the immune system and lead to getting sick. One bout of fierce anger can deplete you energetically for weeks. By learning how to work with your unique elemental type and the strengths that go along with it in your WELL Method and Purpose Plan, you've taken a huge step towards being happy and fulfilling your purpose, and also staying healthy. All of this, just because you're focusing on what you enjoy and what you're good at! There's one common belief that spans most alternative medicine modalities: the human body has the ability to heal itself—of anything—when you rectify imbalances in your constitution. Since your passions, talents, and innate gifts all correspond to your elemental constitution, they are all a part of what keeps the body, mind, and soul healthy. So, go and do what you enjoy!

CHAPTER 8

FACE YOUR FEARS OF CHANGE

Change is the only constant we have in life, yet it can be daunting, intimidating, or downright scary. It's so counterintuitive that we're literally changing every moment of every day, yet it's still difficult to embrace change head-on. In this chapter, we'll discuss the importance of letting go and facing your fears of change so that you can create the purpose-driven life you want.

In the last chapter, we looked at the character development piece that goes along with working with your type. The change that happens from personal growth is a great place to start when facing your fears of change because it happens as a byproduct of pursuing your goals. You're working towards one thing, then you get a direct experience that causes change in your mindset and other parts of your life. Remember, this book is structured sequentially so that you can address getting healthy and living your purpose in the most seamless way possible for body, mind, and soul. Step one was change as a byproduct, resulting from your experience. Step two is consciously initiating change to fuel your goals.

Getting out of your box and trying new things is the first thing I recommend everyone do to start embracing change. The mind is wired to crave consistency. Consistency and habits make us feel good by bringing stability. Change by its nature is not stable and brings in an element of the unknown; in order to remove fear from the unknown, you have to experience it. The unknown brings the possibility of both good and bad experiences, but how you'll relate to the unknown has a lot to do with how you relate to fear. More often than not, new experiences are good ones. The more you move into the unknown and have new, meaningful experiences, the more fear will dissipate, making any sort of change easier.

Making a change in perspective or beliefs is easier than making a big physical change, which makes expanding your horizons and meeting new people less daunting than say, dedicating yourself to a structured exercise practice. There is a reason for this: actions follow thoughts. In order for actions to become fluid and changeable, the mind first has to be fluid and expansive. When the mind becomes acclimated to embracing new things, it becomes possible for your actions to change with much less effort. It's the difference between feeling something is impossible and feeling that it's not only possible, but that you look forward to it. If you can change your mind, you can change your life.

Fear is Always the Wrong Answer

No matter what the situation or decision is, fear is always the wrong answer. Fear is choosing the worst possible outcome of a situation instead of seeing the very real possibility for good. Statistically speaking, you're much more likely to have a positive or neutral reaction to a situation than you are a negative one, and this isn't even taking into account the law of attraction or your mind's ability to create the things it focuses on. What you think about, you will become. What you put your focus on becomes your reality, since actions follow thoughts.

We talked about fear in chapter 5 and how breathing is directly connected to getting rid of fear. Fear constricts the mind and limits our actions. If you don't work to dissipate this energy, fear will stick around in the mind, creating negative thought forms. It's a powerful emotional experience, and any powerful emotional experience needs to be neutralized if you don't want thought forms impacting future decisions. Just as we give power to what we want to create, we must learn to take power away from negative influences. Because fear constricts thoughts towards negative outcomes, persistent fear—or fear mentality—leads to a rigid mindset, which prevents personal growth. A mind riddled with fear can't change or grow or embrace possibility and beauty because it can't see any. It's not possible to expect excellence in yourself when the mind won't allow for change. This type of mindset becomes toxic to you and everyone around you. We discussed many toxic mindsets in the last chapter, including racism, prejudice, nationalism, body shaming, and things that impact other people in a bad way. Don't be that person. Your purpose and a unified mind, body, and soul aren't compatible with a toxic mind.

Choosing love, not fear is the final cornerstone of The WELL Method because your mindset and choices affect more than just you. Every decision will impact numerous other people in some way. It's the butterfly effect, made applicable in your day-to-day life. Even the smallest of decisions can have a profound impact on you or someone else, so why would you ever make a decision that is based on what you think to be the worst possible of all results? We have the collective responsibility to help others in their pursuit of excellence, just as we want to achieve excellence for ourselves. Choosing love positions us and others to receive the best possible outcome of a situation instead of the worst.

So how do you know if a decision is made out of fear? Sometimes it's obvious, others maybe not, but here's a simple way to tell: Is your response to a situation impulsive, negative, or invoking anger? None of those three reactions are coming from a place of love or presence. These are all due to reactive patterns stored in the mind.

Change & Good Health

Why is all of this important from a health perspective? It's due to how energy, chi, or prana, flows in the body. Energy is always moving, just as is blood, lymph, and breath. The body is in a constant state of change and flow. If you stop breathing, you'll die. If you get a blood clot, you may die. If your lymph didn't flow? You guessed it: death. Anything that's not in a constant state of change doesn't have the life force necessary to sustain good health.

Negative emotions slow down the flow of energy in the body, and rigidity of thoughts or beliefs can cause actual energetic blockages. Over time, these start to manifest themselves as physical health problems. Louise Hay did a great job of explaining how our feelings connect to what's happening in the body. And all of this isn't even taking into account the scientifically proven negative effects of stress, sorrow, anger, and sadness on our physical health. We all have good and bad days, and we all deal with negative emotions at some point. Embracing change is the key to keeping the mind, body, and emotions fluid so those experiences don't stick around with us and start causing problems to well-being.

My life has gotten to a point where I don't get sick anymore, which is a huge testament to the power of this work. There's one caveat. If I've gotten into a heated argument that causes anger and intense negative emotions, I'm almost guaranteed to get sick within three days. For a fiery person like me, I've had to learn to not let negative emotions take control, and to do that means I've had to fill my life with a lot of positivity.

We've talked a lot about synergy because the more things that work together, the more positive momentum is built. You can use this momentum to stop fear and other negative emotions in their tracks to readily embrace change in life. It's only when a person feels constricted that change becomes a problem. Fear is the primary culprit, but it can also be due to other negative emotions like sadness, lack of confidence, or anger. Constriction can also come from rationalization or justification of a situation, which is another aspect of a rigid mind. The stronger inner prosperity is, the less likely you are to succumb to fear. It acts as a shield to keep away negativity of all sorts. Even the laws of physics show that momentum builds traction, so apply this to how you live your life. Build momentum. Cultivate inner prosperity daily. Stay consistent with good habits that cultivate excellence in yourself. Do things you enjoy. All of this positive energy helps in embracing change and new opportunities.

When you stay in a flow, you're aligning with the natural rhythms of your body and making it easier to stay well. Holding on to good or bad can cause imbalances because it keeps us from being fully present. The key is in knowing that you'll encounter new experiences every day, and most of them will be good ones. When the bad ones come up, just keep moving until you reach another good experience.

The Turning Point

Embracing change is the turning point for creating the healthy, purpose-filled life you want and, as such, it's the point in the journey where people start to get off-track by not understanding the importance of real change. What does this look like in day-to-day life? What does it mean to change, and how can you recognize it? You know the literal definition and how it's likely to affect the mind and emotions now, so let's take a look at what change really looks like, in a practical sense.

I'll not mince words. When my life really started shifting, there was a lot of unexpected change, especially to my social circle. Old friends started dropping out of communication, and I also got divorced. I was adapting new habits, meditating, being mindful, and this was changing me on a deeper level than I could tell. But others could. My interests were shifting as I was trying new things, and I was putting more time into new endeavors and bettering myself as a person. This can feel threatening to people, because unless you've taken the steps on this journey that we've discussed in the last few chapters, change is scary! The mind is not prepared to deal with it. It's only not scary for the well prepared. I've come to learn from sharing my story that this is a collective experience and not isolated to just me. When you change, your vibrational frequency shifts, which will cause you to fall out of alignment with the people who you were previously aligned with. This is a clear indication that change is happening, and it's a good thing. It may not seem like it at the time, but in order to be successful in your purpose, you have to align yourself with the people and experiences that will be able to support your journey, not hinder it. When one door closes, another will open. This is universal law because the universe abhors a vacuum. You will meet new people and have new experiences that align with your calling, as long as you keep moving forward and embracing change.

Outwardly, it may seem like your life is being thrown into chaos, but it's just realigning with something that suits you better. Inwardly, you'll see some changes too. The most prominent one is that you'll find yourself responding differently to situations (yay for response instead of reaction!). For example, here are some things I noticed in my own life. Let's just start by saying that I have no patience. That's one thing that hasn't changed! Patience may be a virtue, but it's not one of mine, and I'm perfectly fine with that. Seeing as how I lack patience, I used to have a *very* low tolerance to people being late. If someone was late for a meeting or date with me, I'd give the person an earful when they arrived—assuming they arrived before I called the whole thing off and stormed out, which for me was only after waiting about ten minutes. I began to notice when this would happen, and I'd still be upset about it, but I was no longer downright mad. I started giving people a little longer or, if I decided to cancel, I wasn't furious about it like I was before. I just moved on to the next thing without all the emotional baggage of being upset.

After noticing the difference in my reaction, I was able to dive into the thought process behind why it used to bother me at all: I tend towards being early, so the idea of being late was repulsive to me because it meant I was waiting twice as long for someone. I was able to recognize how my actions affected my reaction to the other person, and this knowledge led to even more change. I started letting people know I'd likely arrive a bit early, so they'd be primed for that and be more attentive to not being late. Or, if they knew they were the sort to run late, it would start the conversation allowing them to let me know their routine in a comfortable way.

I also noticed that, in general, I was less likely to be emotionally swayed by things in a way that would let my emotions take control. This meant more and more situations of actively responding to life in the moment. My general level of anger and frustration with my health and life shifted, and after a relatively short period of time, I knew my life had already changed, even though I still had a long way to go and was still working on my health and building a new career. My outer situation had not yet completely changed (it was starting to), but I was different. When it really hit me that I was no longer the same person I was a few months earlier, it was inspiring. It felt strange, but it gave me the motivation to keep pushing forward. It's like you're trudging through mud to get to a grassy meadow. If you look back and realize you've already gone a long way, you're going to keep moving forward because it would be just as much work to turn around and go back to the mess you left as it is to reach your new destination.

Technique to Embrace Change

Now that you're ready to really start making change, let's discuss some ways you can prime the mind to embrace it wholeheartedly. Anytime you accomplish something you've set out to do, it feels great and builds momentum to do it again. So start with small changes. I want you to do at least one thing different each day. It's fine if these things are seemingly random. Maybe this means taking a different route on your walk or commute to work. Maybe it means going for a walk if you don't normally! Maybe it's taking five minutes to sit and breathe on a break from work. Maybe it's trying a new type of tea or coffee! Make it fun and keep it simple so that you can find something new to do each and every day. Keep a journal of all the new things you're doing and a brief note on your reaction to each. This can help you tell how well you're embracing change and when or what situations might make change easier or more difficult. This exercise is helping you build positive neural connections that will train your mind to not only enjoy change but also to look forward to it each and every day.

You'll probably find a few things you don't like, and a lot of it will be neutral with no real emotional impact, but I bet you'll discover some new things that really bring meaning to your life and lead to a lasting change. You never know what you'll discover when you expand your horizons.

CHAPTER 9

FOOD FOR MOOD & WELL-BEING

Food is so much more than fuel to give your body energy. It has the power to make you mentally healthy or unstable, keep your emotions healthy and elevated, put you on a roller-coaster of wild ups and downs, or even directly heal the physical body or cause disease in it. Quite literally, you are what you eat, and I'm not the only one who thinks so. Dr. David Friedman, author of *Food Sanity* and host of *To Your Good Health Radio*, says, "You are what you eat. Every day, billions of cells in the human body die and get replaced with new ones. The building blocks for every cell in our body come from the food we consume." In terms of an actual superpower you can cultivate, wisely choosing what you eat is at the top of the list.

Dr. Josh Axe has a very personal story around food and its medicinal benefits. Here's what he told me: "Despite my mother, who was a Phys Ed teacher and swim coach, being considered 'healthy' by most standards for the majority of her life, she was diagnosed with stage four breast cancer about twenty years ago.

"She initially underwent a mastectomy followed by many rounds of chemotherapy, which thankfully were successful but also had a lasting impact on her health by contributing to many unwanted symptoms such as digestive issues, candida, depression, and chronic fatigue syndrome. After she was diagnosed with cancer for a second time, she decided to pursue natural cancer treatments and to focus on improving her diet and lifestyle in order to heal.

"Her protocol included eating an anti-inflammatory diet that emphasized lots of fresh vegetables (including fresh, raw juices), beef liver, and probiotic foods, as well taking immune-boosting supplements like digestive enzymes and vitamin D, thyroid hormones, and frankincense oil, detoxifying with the help of enemas and chelation, working on reducing stress, praying, and staying active. My mom was able to once again overcome her disease and has remained cancer-free ever since. We believe she was able to recover thanks to a *combination* of both conventional medical treatments and a healthy lifestyle/natural remedies."

Stories like this one around remarkable healing experiences are ones I've heard time and time again. If you change your diet, you can change just about anything in your life, including mental, emotional, and physical health. I deeply believe this as it's been my own personal experience as well. Because of the profound impact that food has not only on physical health but also mental and emotional health, I believe that food insecurity is one of the most detrimental problems our society is facing. Few people know this better than musician and legend, Jon Bon Jovi. His JBJ Soul Kitchen currently operates three locations in New Jersey (they recently opened a location in Rutgers University) where people can choose what they pay for a meal based on what they are able to contribute. No one is turned away, even if they cannot afford to pay.

Food & Mind-Body-Soul Wellness

Food is unequivocally your best medicine, and your relationship with it will determine how healthy, harmonized, and balanced your entire life is. Food will make or break your relationship with yourself, as it's either going to be your most valuable ally or your worst enemy. Food is the single most important factor to your health and well-being. I'd like to say the single most important factor in wellness is mindfulness and meditation, but people don't have to be mindful. We have free will and mindfulness is a conscious choice; eating food is not. If you don't consume food and water, you will die. Given that we have to eat to survive, why do more people not eat to thrive?

Nutritional psychology is an emerging field looking at the psychological connections between food and mood, but Ayurveda and TCM are anything but new and have long understood the connection of food to mood, mindfulness, and good health. Ayurveda, in fact, sees healthy digestion as the primary factor in health and that improperly digested foods are the root of all disease. This is why eating for your unique elemental type is important, because it's not just about the foods themselves but how quickly your body digests the food you eat and how much energy the body has to expend on digestion. Eating to your type optimizes this process. The fire element is what controls digestion, and it's also what controls willpower, motivation, and self-confidence. The fire element is at the root of self-inquiry. It's also what keeps you sharp, agile, focused, and in control of your life. If your inner fire is being used mostly on digestion, you won't have the energy left to fuel the rest of your endeavors or create the life you want.

Food and your relationship with it is a foundational tool for wellness that can be used at every stage in cultivating health—from the most basic aspects of getting the right nutrient balance, to working with your unique elemental type to optimize digestion, health, and performance, all the way to the highly specialized approaches of using food to regulate your mood, emotions, and mental health. I'm a huge advocate of it all, but especially using food for mood and mental health, and understanding how it either benefits or depletes your elemental constitution.

Food, Digestion & Your Elemental Type

I consider eating to your unique type and improving digestion as foundational for optimizing performance and mental agility. This helps bring your elemental attributes into harmony so the body can function at its best. Remember that earth and water types are apt to get bogged down and sluggish more easily than fire or air types, meaning that eating lighter, less calorie-dense foods during the day can help optimize their performance. Air types in particular can have problems with spaciness and stability, meaning they need heavier, grounding foods to function well, like root vegetables, fish, tempeh, or calorie-dense meals. Note, I'm not talking about a burger and fries; I'm talking about healthy choices that match your elemental profile. Eating the right foods can eliminate a problem or mitigate it completely before it arises.

Adjusting your food consumption in terms of amounts and types based on how you're feeling is a good place to start. You can expand on this by ensuring you're keeping your inner fire element as strong as it can be, regardless of your primary elemental type. One way to do this is to space your meals apart by approximately four hours, which means no snacking. There are diverse opinions on this, but the elemental-based approach is to avoid it. Some people say they need to snack to regulate blood sugar, but this is a misconception; the body does a better job with regulation of all bodily functions when it's not constantly using the fire element to digest food. Remember, fire is also necessary to digest thoughts and experiences, and to cultivate strong willpower and self-confidence.

Another key to keeping digestion strong is to balance food and fluid intake. It takes the fire element to digest food, but the water element dampens the fire element. In other words, don't drink fluids at the same time you are eating a meal. Have them thirty minutes or more in advance or during that three to four hour period between your meals. This simple trick alone will change your relationship with food, guaranteed.

In people for whom fire is not a dominant element in their elemental type (everyone has all elements, but it may not be your strong one), spicy foods can upset the balance. If you don't relate well to spicy, don't eat much of it because it'll cause problems with digestion. Speaking of spicy, do you find yourself prone to anger? Cut back on spicy foods, as this is assured to aggravate

Figure 9-1: common lifestyle problems & their food-based solutions.

Problem	Food Solution
Anger	Avoid spicy foods.
Poor memory	Walnuts, broccoli, turmeric, blueberries, fatty fish, cacao.
Depression	Turmeric + black pepper, cashew, saffron.
Anxiety or nerves	Ginger, tea, asafetida, cumin.
Stress, negative emotions	Asafetida (hing), chard, bananas.
Upset stomach	Ginger, cardamom, star anise.
Inflammation	Turmeric + black pepper, saffron, berries, green tea.
Constipation	Fiber-rich foods (apples, pears, leafy greens, etc.), flaxseed, kiwi.
Diarrhea	Bananas, oatmeal, rice.
Physical pain	Ginger, turmeric, olive oil, saffron, fenugreek, star anise, chili peppers.

anger and make it worse. Since anger is a sign of an unbalanced fire element, bringing it back to balance will improve not only your mood but also digestion. Here are some more food-based solutions to common problems you may be dealing with.

Food for Mood & Well-being

My daily diet is focused around keeping my mood elevated and boosting energy levels so I can go, go, go. After dealing with fibromyalgia and healing from it, daily fatigue and sorrow is something I never want to experience again, and thankfully, food is a simple and powerful solution. Certain foods cause biochemical reactions in the body, triggering neurotransmitters like dopamine, serotonin, and norepinephrine, all of which help regulate mood and promote happy feelings. Low levels of dopamine and serotonin are linked to depression, apathy, loss of satisfaction, boredom, and a general decline in mood. Increasing serotonin is akin to happy relaxation (it can make you a bit drowsy) whereas increasing dopamine can improve motivation and an active sort of happy energy to keep you going. Both are important for good health.

Foods can also have adverse effects on health and well-being, including causing inflammation, a decline in cognitive function and memory, and other serious diseases like high blood pressure, type 2 diabetes, heart disease, osteoporosis, and even some types of cancer. Chronic inflammation in the body is at the root of many problems, including heart disease, stroke, many auto-immune diseases, and other chronic conditions like fibromyalgia, rheumatoid arthritis, and lupus. Anyone dealing with chronic inflammation is recommended to eat an anti-inflammatory diet to reduce symptoms and pain, but inflammation does more than cause pain; it's also been identified as a major contributing factor of depression. It's long been known that the anti-inflammatory superfood turmeric helps elevate mood and decrease depression, but direct scientific evidence of the role of inflammation in depression is a relatively recent discovery. That discovery had not been made by science when I was dealing with fibromyalgia, but thankfully, the mind-body wellness communities were well aware of turmeric and its benefits, which was very helpful for me.

Tryptophan-containing foods are a great example of mood-boosting foods since tryptophan metabolizes to produce serotonin in the body. Tryptophan is the infamous compound turkey is well known for that causes drowsiness after a large, turkey-filled Thanksgiving dinner. Cheese and dairy in general also contain tryptophan, which may be why so many people like dairy! Before you up your cheese or milk intake though, I'd recommend getting your source of tryptophan from other foods because dairy products can cause adverse reactions. Nearly 65 percent of the global population is believed to be lactose intolerant, and high-fat dairy products have been directly linked to an increase in inflammation in the body. You can get tryptophan from seeds, nuts, salmon, poultry, eggs, spinach, and soy products. Given there are so many choices, I'd recommend avoiding dairy products altogether when creating your mood-boosting diet, and definitely avoiding it if you are on an anti-inflammatory diet.

If you want foods to boost your energy and motivation while elevating mood, I'd go for ones that increase dopamine production in the body. My favorite in this group is the superfood cacao; it's where dark chocolate comes from. I go straight for the cacao because it's low in calories and contains no dairy, unlike most chocolate. Cacao is one of the few things I consume daily because of its potent mind, body, and spirit benefits. Chocolate is God and Goddess food, quite literally—the cacao tree's scientific name is Theobroma cacao, which directly translates to "cacao, food of the Gods." It boosts mood; increases energy, stamina, focus, memory, and mental agility; is a natural aphrodisiac; and also opens people up to their creative and spiritual sides. It's mind, body, and spirit food at its best, and it's used in some spiritual traditions as a means of worship. Making and drinking cacao as a means of worship and prayer helps people connect with all of its mind, body, and soul benefits.

Eating foods that help increase and support neurotransmitter function in the body has long been a part of spiritual tradition, and not just in relation to cacao. We all have limited time each day, making something practical and necessary like eating food a great way to support mind, body, and soul. It helps us remember that the seemingly simple and mundane parts of life are never as mundane as they seem. We can use anything and everything as a way to experience God and strengthen our sense of purpose in life. Eating mood-boosting foods helps people maintain the positivity needed to stay connected with one's highest self and God. A good mood equates to a higher vibrational frequency, more inner prosperity, openness, expansiveness, and a closer-felt connection with God.

There are many great dopamine producing foods in addition to cacao, including bananas, nuts, omega-3's (think salmon, mackerel, flaxseed, hempseed, walnuts, etc.), seaweed, and chia seeds. Since dopamine is directly connected to motivation levels and willpower, it can help build your spiritual connection and create positive momentum while helping the fire element do its job on a mental and emotional level.

Morning is a great time to get lots of these mood-boosting foods into your routine. My morning meal is no joke. I consider it my most important meal of the day because it sets the stage for how the entire day goes and fuels my exercise routine. If I'm forced to have a less than optimal breakfast for any reason, my entire day suffers from it. I'm not as mentally alert or prepared to deal with stress, my energy levels are lower, and my mood is off. Most mornings, I make a dairy-free, protein-packed, pre and probiotic, mood-boosting smoothie for breakfast that incorporates cacao, nut milk, peanut butter, bananas, and other superfoods. If I want hot food instead, I go for a healing spice-based quinoa, kale, and egg combo.

By eating a good variety of foods that stimulate your mind, body, and spirit while working with your elemental type, you are helping to manifest the best possible version of yourself each and every day. Expecting excellence of yourself is something you have to wake up each day and choose, again and again. Your food choices make it much easier to be the best you imaginable. With some experimentation, you can create some mood-boosting meals that'll optimize your day, based on your unique needs and lifestyle.

The Gut-Brain Connection

A mindful approach to food is a must if you want to continue on your journey towards purpose and health, and understanding the gut-brain connection will inspire your mindfulness with food even more. The gut-brain connection starts with the microbiome that lives in the gut; it's comprised of trillions of cells and microorganisms including bacteria, fungi, and even viruses that are a crucial part of our health and well-being. Humans are born with these microbes, and this symbiotic relationship has a potent effect on our brain; behaviors; and anatomical, physiological, and immunological development as we grow. Humans have so many microbes on the skin and in the body that they outnumber our own cells ten to one. In fact, the microbes in your gut alone can account for about four pounds of your body weight!

You may have seen in the news the past couple of years about the gut's microbiome and its connection to obesity in people lacking certain critical strains of microbes. It's not just the amount but also their variety that's important to well-being. To make this discussion of microbes even more exciting, Dr. Friedman says, "The gut is often referred to as the 'second brain' because it has its own enteric nervous system that works independently of our cerebrum. The gut helps in our decision making, hence the terms 'trust your gut' and 'what's your gut instinct telling you?'" If you think about it, since these microorganisms outnumber our own cells ten to one, it's no surprise they have a major impact on our psychology and behavior. A depleted microbiome can cause anxiety, stress, fear, and depression in people.

Having healthy intestinal flora has a host of physical health benefits too. "When the flora doesn't function properly, this can lead to food intolerance, obesity, irritable bowel syndrome, auto-immune disease, depression, thyroid disease, and even cancer," says Dr. Friedman. The key to healthy flora has three main physical parts: prebiotics, probiotics, and eliminating chemicals and additives found in processed foods. Probiotics are the flora themselves; you can buy probiotic foods and supplements to help boost the amount and variety of beneficial microbes in your gut. Probiotic foods include yogurt with cultures, kefir, sauerkraut, kimchi, kombucha, and other fermented foods and drinks.

Before you start consuming more probiotics, make sure you're getting enough prebiotics. This is what most people either aren't aware of or forget to do. Prebiotics are the nutrients your gut microbiome feeds on that keep it healthy and thriving. What good is taking probiotics if they die in your gut because they don't get the proper nourishment? Fiber is an important prebiotic, making it extra important to health. A few great sources of prebiotic fiber include chicory root, dandelion greens, Jerusalem artichokes, garlic, onions, leeks, bananas, oats, asparagus, barley, apples, and flaxseed.

Limiting processed foods that contain chemical additives is just as important as consuming pre- and probiotics because chemical additives can kill the flora in your gut, leading to the health problems mentioned above. A simple rule of thumb is: if you can't pronounce an ingredient in your food or don't know what it is, you probably shouldn't be eating it. Additives are found in most processed foods. Chemicals can find their way into food through the cookware you use and the containers food is stored in. Avoiding aluminum-based and non-stick cookware is a good start, as is avoiding plastic storage containers.

A fourth major component of gut health is your emotional state. Prolonged stress, anxiety, negative emotions, and anger can all kill your intestinal flora. Even if you're doing everything else to support gut health, if you're not managing your stress levels and emotions, your gut flora will suffer from it, causing a host of possible physical and mental health problems that we've discussed. Here's what's really interesting: stress and anxiety can kill your flora, but having a depleted flora can also cause stress and anxiety, meaning that it goes both ways. Taking care of the physical body is just as important as taking care of your mental and emotional health.

When the gut's microbiome gets killed for any reason, it causes issues with digestion, which brings us back to how we started this chapter, discussing the importance of a strong digestion to health and well-being. Could it be that the ancient sages who developed Ayurveda had an understanding of the microbiome? If they didn't, they at least knew bad digestion leads to bad health.

Spice is Twice as Nice

We can't talk about food without discussing the role of spices. Add some spice to your cooking routine, because nearly all spices have some medicinal and mood-boosting quality to them. Spices are an extremely powerful healing tool to add to your repertoire; you can change your health with them without drastically modifying the actual foods you eat. You can use spices as a natural and complementary way to treat nearly any health condition and to elevate mood. Here are some ways that common spices have been used in alternative medicine to improve well-being. Oh, are you a fan of the holiday season? Every holiday spice has potent medicinal benefits, as you'll see below.

Figure 9-2: common spices & their medicinal benefits.

Spice	Medicinal and Healing Qualities
Asafetida	Prevents and treats asthma, bronchitis, and whooping cough, antispasmotic, expectorant, laxative, sedative, lowers blood pressure, treats IBS, helps regulate blood sugar, used to treat hysteria.
Black pepper	Improves digestion, reduces gas and bloating, diuretic, high in fiber, improves cognitive function, antioxidant, increases bioavailability of nutrients in food, antibacterial, aids weight loss by breaking down fat cells, treats peptic ulcers, anti-inflammatory, expectorant, relieves respiratory problems including asthma.
Cardamom	Antidepressant, improves heart health, improves GI health, anti-inflammatory, anti-spasmotic, improves oral health, decreases asthma symptoms, detoxifies the body, improves blood circulation, treats nausea, sore throat, and vomiting, rich in vitamins, antimicrobial, helps prevent cancer, reduces diabetes, diuretic, enhances appetite, lowers blood pressure, improves sexual health, improves skin complexion.
Cloves	Antioxidant, antibacterial, antiviral, improves liver health, regulates blood sugar, improves bone health, anti-inflammatory, regulates hunger levels, treats tooth pain.
Cinnamon	Antioxidant, anti-inflammatory, improves heart health, lowers blood sugar, promotes memory, lowers cancer risk, antibacterial, antiviral, antimicrobial, prevents cavities and bad breath, boosts immunity, prevents and eliminates candida, can treat skin irritations, rashes, fights allergies, natural food preservative.
Coriander	Lowers blood sugar, prevents stomach disorders, decreases blood pressure, combats food poisoning, promotes eye health, prevents anemia, reduces histamine-related allergies, antimicrobial, antioxidant, improves cholesterol, lowers high blood pressure, treats UTIs, supports healthy menstruation, reduces inflammation in the skin.
Cumin	Aids in digestion, boosts immune system, treats respiratory disorders, good for skin by preventing premature aging, treats insomnia, may prevent diabetes, antibacterial, antiviral, improves cognitive performance, laxative, improves lactation, relieves anxiety and stress, eliminates mucus and phlegm.
Fennel	Improves bone health, lowers blood pressure, boosts immunity, anti-inflammatory, weight management, increases iron absorption.
Fenugreek	Promotes healthy lactation, reduces menstrual cramps, minimizes menopause symptoms, reduces heart problems, lowers cholesterol, natural laxative, treats kidney problems, suppresses appetite, aids digestion and metabolism, reduces fever, reduces muscle aches.
Garlic	Boosts immunity and restores suppressed antibody response, antiviral, reduces blood pressure, lowers cholesterol, antioxidant, reduces fatigue, may reduce Alzheimer's and dementia, detoxes heavy metals from the body, reduces signs of metal toxicity including headaches and high blood pressure, improves athletic performance.
Ginger	Boosts memory, concentration, reaction time and attention to detail, may combat Alzheimer's and dementia, powerful antioxidant, anti-inflammatory, pain reducer, decreases nausea, settles nerves, treats chronic indigestion, decreases menstrual pain, increases insulin sensitivity and lowers blood sugar levels, reduces adrenal fatigue, antiviral, lowers cholesterol.
Red chili pepper	Promotes heart health, relieves joint pain, reduces migraines, good for digestive tract health, improves metabolism and promotes weight loss, treats psoriasis, antiviral, antifungal, anti-inflammatory.
Nutmeg	Reduces pain, treats insomnia, improves digestion, improves memory and concentration, reduces depression, reduces anxiety, reduces blood pressure, treats bad breath, improves skin complexion.
Star anise	Antiviral, improves digestion, reduces nausea, reduces stomach cramps, reduces bloating and gas, relieves constipation, improves sex drive.

Tips to Boost Mood & Mental Health

You already have a whole arsenal of advice in this chapter, so let's start putting it into practice by cultivating mindful eating. Mindful eating goes beyond *what* you eat, to *how* you eat. Are you distracted during meals? Maybe you work through your lunch breaks or sit down to watch TV during dinner with the family. You can change your relationship with food permanently by adding mindfulness to it. Be fully present with your meals, without distraction. Bringing attention to the act of eating can even help you eat less and feel fuller. This means you'll consume fewer calories each day, which is a good thing because research shows that people underestimate how many calories they consume each day by roughly 20–40 percent. Mindful eating is an effective way to skip calorie counting and still be in tune with what your body and mind need to succeed.

The more sensory experiences you can connect to eating, the more quickly you'll feel satisfied and full. This includes smell, taste, appearance and plating, how food feels in your mouth while you're eating it, and hearing yourself chew. You'll not notice these things if you're distracted, but through creating a mindful eating experience, you can tune into all of them.

Step #1: Sit and eat your meal with no distractions and bring attention to all five sensory perceptions. I'd recommend putting slightly less food on your plate than normal, as you'll quickly notice that you feel fuller with less food. Try to have at least one mindful meal each day while you're creating your new routine.

Step #2: Let's now take your new mindful eating experience a step further. Structure a day of mindful eating where you're getting each of these in your diet:

- three mood-boosting foods that produce dopamine or serotonin
- one prebiotic food
- one probiotic food
- two types of fruit
- two types of vegetables
- two medicinal spices
- limit processed foods
- limit refined sugars

Your food choices will likely fall into more than one of these categories at the same time. Ideally, you'll be consuming lots more fruits and vegetables than what I've listed above, but making realistic and attainable goals is the best way to start being mindful. Note, this mentions limiting processed foods and refined sugars. Processed foods are a primary culprit of additives and chemicals in food, and refined sugars do more damage to your health than I have time to explain here. I'll keep it simple by saying the more you eat whole, nutrient-dense foods without preservatives, refined sugars, additives or colorings, the healthier you mind, mood, and body will be.

CHAPTER 10

LET'S SHAKE IT! (THE POWER OF EXERCISE)

Since mind, body, and soul are three parts of the same whole, when you affect one of those pieces, the others are also affected. Up to this point, we've focused on ways to optimize mental and emotional health to facilitate physical well-being because thoughts and feelings are the foundation for good health and a successful, purpose-driven life. Here is where we start working with the body to facilitate physical health and also support mental and emotional well-being. This technically started with the last chapter, although arguably food has more to do with a healthy mind and emotional state than most people give it credit for.

Exercise is what most people think of when they think about wellness, but in reality, it's only a piece of the larger picture, and it's a piece that is extremely misunderstood in terms of its impact. Most people believe that weight loss or gain is determined mostly by exercise or lack of it, but that is not true. It's mostly based on diet, caloric intake, and how well you're eating to your elemental type. Many people also believe that intense exercise is best for the body, but again, this is untrue. What you need is unique to you, and it may well be something more moderate or low impact. What exercise *does* do is play a role in reducing hunger levels, getting better sleep, reducing pain in the body, boosting dopamine production and energy levels, getting your energy (prana) moving, and helping you hone skills based on your elemental type. I'm a huge advocate of picking activities in life that support multiple aspects of well-being. When you know how to approach exercise, it can do much more than just get your blood pumping. It's a great way to utilize your strengths to build more confidence, cultivate inner prosperity, and expect excellence in yourself.

Just like with mindfulness, the key to success with exercise is to find something that you can stay consistent with, and that will be based on how you approach it and what your unique goals are. First, let's get out of the box of thinking about the gym or weights or running. Those may be good options, but there are so many more. If you had to pick just one simple thing to do for exercise, I'd suggest walking. The physical health benefits alone are staggering: it boosts immunity, raises energy levels, eases joint pain, is good for the heart, can lower blood sugar levels, tones the legs, and is a great exercise for weight loss. Walking also boosts mood by increasing dopamine production in the body and spurs creative thinking. All of this, and it's something most people can do with minimal effort or exertion, meaning you are more likely to stay consistent with it. Let's use this chapter as a way to redefine how you look at physical activity and how it can benefit the whole you.

Exercise & Your Personality

Try approaching physical activity by finding something that matches your temperament and elemental type. When you do this, you benefit multiple parts of the mind-body-soul connection at the same time and can use exercise as a way to strengthen your unique talents while building confidence in yourself. If you have combined earth and space elements, you'll probably really enjoy dancing. Combined air and fire types often have a fondness for running. Water types, you might like swimming or group exercise classes most of all. Earth and fire types, you may gravitate towards aerobics, HIIT, and weight training. There's no right or wrong in what you try, but with a bit of effort, you will find what is right for you.

Let's say that you have a personal goal to increase your creativity and put yourself in inspirational settings. You can use exercise as a way to do this. Things like yoga, tai chi, dancing, or even fencing may be a way to get moving and get creative at the same time. Maybe your goal is to blow off steam and aggression at the end of the day so you don't take that toxic energy home into your personal relationships. You may find that boxing or martial arts is a great fit for you and a way to channel that energy productively. Do you have a highly analytical job and want to balance your right and left brain? Try an exercise that involves balance and grounding like yoga or tai chi.

Your elemental type plays a role in how much stamina and energy you'll have, so picking types of exercise that don't leave you depleted is an important factor to consider. Part of maintaining inner prosperity is learning how to always feel you have more than enough—be it stamina, energy, or positivity. Air and space types will tend to have much less stamina than fire, water, or earth types. As we've discussed, air types also benefit from more grounding endeavors, while water and earth types will benefit from getting active to remove inertia. As an earth and fire type, I tend to have a lot of stamina, and I use part of it to keep moving and active throughout the day so as to not build up inertia in the mind or body. Stagnation in the mind is no good for being a writer, so I know that for me to be my best each day, several periods of activity throughout the day are what keep me feeling at my best. This makes walking a great primary choice, and not doing overly intense workouts so I can keep going all day. I also add in a couple days each of cardio and weight training to keep building stamina and confidence. As an earthy type, I also really enjoy dance, but this is harder to be consistent with because I can't do it on my own time, nor can I find a morning dance class.

Time of day factors into when movement may benefit you most. For earth and water types, starting the day off active sets the stage for having sustained energy throughout the day since it helps remove the extra inertia we get from sleep and provides energy. Fire and air types may prefer to be active mid-day or evening since they don't have to combat as much inertia and so they can get grounded before settling into sleep. Since an earth type can get energized from exercise, nighttime workouts could interfere with healthy sleep due to their energizing effect. So even though I love dancing, it's not the best choice for me since night-time classes keep me from having restful sleep. Find what works for you to optimize your lifestyle and daily routines.

What's your type and what are your goals? How will this inform your decision about the best way to approach a consistent exercise routine? It's the consistency that helps build confidence, and there are few better ways to cultivate confidence than to see what you are physically capable of doing.

Exercise & Character Development

Food and exercise are the two most powerful physical means of changing your mindset to the positive and cultivating belief in yourself. The reasons food and exercise are so powerful for accomplishing your goals go far beyond boosting dopamine and confidence; they enable the body to function at its peak performance, which is necessary for the mind, soul, and emotions to be at their peak performance because—let's say this together—mind, body, and soul are three parts of the same whole.

The human body is built to be active, so the more you engage with the physical body and keep it active, the easier it is to connect with your soul and to feel empowered to fulfill your purpose. Action all happens through the body. Literally everything that we do requires the physical body to get it done. Every time you do something, you are connecting the flow of energy from thought to action to accomplishment, which completes the process of manifestation. Not being physically able to take an action necessary to manifest your ideas stops the flow of energy and prevents that purpose-driven life you're creating. Lacking skill to accomplish an action is one thing—you can always learn new skills. The most common limiting factor in reaching your goals is the body not having the energy, stamina, or confidence to get things done, or downright not being healthy enough to reach your goal.

Low stamina and energy in the body equate to low confidence and willpower in the mind. When you lack physical endurance, you also tend to lack mental endurance, and this can diminish what you believe you're able to accomplish. Daily exercise helps to build endurance and get energy flowing in both the body and mind. Even the simple act of walking spurs creative thought. When energy is no longer stagnant due to inactivity, it flows freely, making it accessible wherever it's needed in the body or mind. What might have felt impossible before may feel entirely possible when you're in a clearer frame of mind. My own experience has shown me that if I don't stay active every day, there is a noticeable difference in what I feel I can accomplish. If I go more than a couple days without exercise, my entire frame of mind shifts in an unhelpful and unhealthy way, where I no longer believe I can do everything I know I am capable of. Even if your diet is in order, lack of movement will impact how you perceive your own abilities and how you respond to situations life throws at you.

Let's look at strength. Strength comes from resistance. You don't build strength by being inactive in mind, body, or soul. You build strength and stamina by constantly pushing yourself to new limits. When you push your body to get stronger, your mind becomes stronger in the process. The more you work with your body, the more you are cultivating these same skills in your mind and emotions. Strength, stamina, willpower, perseverance, and courage can all be cultivated just by working with the physical body and keeping it active and healthy. If you're the sort of person who juggles multiple priorities, exercise will help you keep all those plates in the air without any breaking. If you're dealing with physical or emotional trauma, exercise can help you cope better and heal more quickly. Being a survivor of sexual abuse, I take the body-mind connection very seriously. You can't heal trauma locked in the mind and body through thought alone. Healing comes from overwriting painful memories by having new experiences. The more the body is used to cultivate strength and confidence, the easier it is for the body memory to let go of the past.

The quickest way to use exercise to strengthen your stamina and willpower is to work with your core, a.k.a. your stomach muscles. A strong core is central to a strong and healthy body and mind. Try doing the plank pose daily. It strengthens all the abdominal muscles, not just the top ones that sit-ups affect, and it will also strengthen your lower and mid back, arms, and chest muscles. You don't need fancy machines, just your own body weight. Start with as little as fifteen seconds at a time depending on your current activity level and work your way up. Do this daily for two weeks each morning and see how you feel, assuming of course you have no physical or health conditions that would prevent this from being a safe exercise for you. I love simple things like this because everyone has an extra minute in their day. This may be simple (not easy), but even just a minute a day done consistently will add up to huge changes in your strength and stamina quickly, and you will notice how these changes improve your relationship with yourself.

Flexibility is also important to discuss because a flexible body helps to cultivate flexibility and reduce stress in the mind and emotions. Rigidity of thought and beliefs is one of the things that holds people back in life. Being able to adapt, analyze your thoughts and beliefs, and change them when you need to is a key to growth. By making flexibility a focus of your exercise routine, you are also strengthening this skill in your mind and making it easier to alleviate stress, to grow, and to change. Stretching exercises are the best way to remain flexible in body and mind, and they have the added benefit of making you feel good. If you have a desk job, make sure to get up, stretch, and move around frequently.

Strength, stamina, endurance, flexibility, and self-confidence are all hallmarks of character development, and that is not something you can work on in and of itself. It's reflected in how you respond to life and how you feel about yourself. Exercise is a great tool for developing character because it helps you realize what you are capable of. Keep pushing yourself to new limits and watch how it helps you fulfill your purpose in life. And remember, you don't have to work out an hour or more a day. For mind-body wellness, it's more important to be consistent with a routine than it is to make it long and drawn out.

I want to be clear here that I am not saying if you have a disability, you are doomed or are somehow not going to be able to live your purpose or cultivate confidence. People with physical disabilities who learn how to overcome their limitations shine more brightly than the average person. We all have some form of limitation, and that is not the obstacle. The obstacle is when you limit yourself by not properly taking care of the whole you, mind, body, and soul. The mind knows when limitations are self-imposed due to neglect, and it will hinder what you set out to accomplish because you are the one responsible for limiting yourself. It's a self-fulfilling prophecy. You probably don't consciously realize when you're limiting yourself, which is why learning to expect excellence is a powerful tool for changing the subconscious mind, enabling you to get out of your own way. If you're baking a cake and you don't use the right ingredients, you're not going to end up making a cake, or something in it will taste off. This is the same for life: if you don't fill your life with the right ingredients to build inner and outer prosperity, strength, and perseverance, you're not going to end up creating the life you want.

The Body-Soul Connection

Exercising, eating clean, healthy foods, and keeping the physical body in good shape has profound positive effects on your mind and emotions, but it may have an even more profound effect on your spiritual connection and your ability to believe that God is a living part of you. The body-soul connection is often the weakest link in the mind-body-soul triad and is well worth your effort to strengthen because this connection is the one that makes the real you visible to the world. Think about your physical body as the soul made visible. Since your soul's purpose created everything about your temperament, talents, and physical body structure, your body is nothing less than your soul manifested visibly in human form.

Spiritual connection is felt through your emotions, and you see it in yourself and others through the physical body. Have you ever looked at someone and just knew instantly they were a wonderful person? Or the opposite, when you feel creeped out by just seeing someone? The connection you've cultivated with the God inside of you is visible to others, both consciously and subconsciously. It is said the eyes are the gateway to the soul; when you look into someone's eyes, you can know a lot about their relationship with God and themselves.

If you think about the body as the temple of God and truly honor it as such, what would this change in your life? Would it change the way you relate to yourself or others? The concept of embodiment of divinity, recognizing and nurturing the God within you, is found in both Eastern spiritual traditions and Christianity. I don't want to call this a belief, because it's actually a relationship with yourself, with God, and with your unlimited highest potential. Cultivating a personal relationship with God puts a very strong emphasis on taking care of the physical body because it is the only one you get to live your purpose and to deepen your spiritual connection through. What does this relationship mean to you? When you look in the mirror, do you see the God that resides inside of you? If not, what do you see?

Spirituality is not a belief in God but an experience of God and a relationship with your highest self. If this concept remains confined only to your thoughts or beliefs, you'll miss out on actually experiencing the divinity that resides within you. Thinking of something is a form of observing it. Embodying something makes it your direct experience, and this is how you gain wisdom and how you're able to apply it in day-to-day life. We talked about action earlier and how important action is for cultivating self-confidence and mental stamina. Action through the form of exercise is the body's way of communicating with the soul and strengthening the body-soul connection.

Connections in the mind-body-soul triad go both ways, but the best way for the body to communicate with the mind (or soul) is not necessarily the best way for the mind (or soul) to communicate with the body. Strengthening the connections from both sides will help you live your purpose and encounter fewer obstacles along the way.

Figure 10-1: ways to strengthen the individual connections between body, mind & soul.

Action	Connection Strengthened
Eating Food	Body → Mind
Exercise	Body → Soul
Mindfulness	Mind → Body
Meditation	Mind → Soul
Prayer & Intention Setting	Soul → Mind
Worship	Soul → Body
Living Your Purpose	Soul → Mind & Body

The first thing that comes to mind for most people when thinking about the body-soul connection is yoga, but you can use any form of physical activity to strengthen your body-soul connection. The key is to find what makes you feel good physically, mentally, and emotionally and to find what you're able to commit to and stay consistent with. Now, let's get moving!

CHAPTER 11

SPEAK NO EVIL (THE POWER OF WORDS)

The power of the spoken word is something inspiring and downright beautiful to behold. When you speak something, you are taking an idea from your mind and, for the first time, beginning to make that thought into a tangible reality. Because speech is a direct bridge from thought to reality, learning to use your words effectively can increase what you're able to accomplish and strongly impact how you feel about yourself. In this chapter, you'll learn how to shape a positive, believable, and healthy dialogue to yourself and others that supports your purpose, health, and life goals.

Mind, Body & Soul Connection to Sound

There are few things as inspiring in life as the way music can move and uplift your soul. Pleasant music, nature sounds, or someone telling you they love you all have a rejuvenative effect that works on all layers of the mind, body, and soul at once. The power of sound is such that it doesn't work with one part of the triad then affect the others—mind, body, and soul all feel the effects at the same time. Think about what happens when you hear some really upbeat music. Your mind shifts to the positive. Your body probably starts moving to the beat. Your energy levels increase, and you feel more optimistic, all at the same time. For me, music, mantra, and the power of speech was very important to my healing journey and changing my beliefs about what I thought I could or could not accomplish. Because it works on all layers at once, sound provides an instant platform of stability to anchor to and grow from.

This ability to work with the whole you at once shows the tremendous power of sound and what makes the things you say out loud a real part of your life. The sound current connects to the sense of hearing and space element and, as a sensory perception, is part of the physical world. Mystics from both Eastern and Western religions have spoken of the connection of sound to God. According to both the Upanishads and the Bible, sound was the first thing created in the material world. The Bible says, "In the beginning there was the Word, and the Word was God." The Upanishads say something very similar about all of existence stemming from the sound current. From the sound current, the rest of life and everything in the physical world was created, including the other four elements.

This is important, because it means that vibrational frequency is part of all things and that sound has a powerful effect on all things, no matter how dense and material they are. Being the piece of creation born directly from God, it's no wonder that sound holds such healing, creative and destructive power, and also the power to manifest anything you want to create in life. Being the bridge between thought and action, sound can be used directly on a mental, emotional, and spiritual level to elevate your life and help change your habits and thoughts.

Motivation and self-confidence can be made or broken by the things you say to yourself or by what others say to you. Sound is alive; since it's a living part of God, we have the responsibility to use words wisely. Let's do a small exercise. Take a moment to think: what was the last thing you said to yourself, about yourself? I want you to write it down on a piece of paper.

If what you said was something positive, kudos to you! Fold this paper up and put it in your purse or wallet. If what you said was not something beneficial, cross it out and write something positive about yourself instead. Now keep this paper with you for the next few weeks. Take it out each day and reflect on your words. That paper, whether you originally wrote something good or bad, represents a turning point where you now know the power of speech and will hopefully commit to making your words positive and productive. By committing to carrying it with you, you'll feel the impact that speech has on your mood, motivation levels, and inner prosperity.

Take a moment to think about what you wrote and why. I want you to write down your reasons why here. I know I'm asking you to do something hard, and that is part of the point. Our inner dialogue, which turns into our outer dialogue, comes from deeply held thought patterns and feelings. You probably didn't have a clear reason behind what you wrote unless it was due to a recent occurrence.

When you reflect on your why, was it a real reason based on a tangible occurrence, an inner dialogue you've been telling yourself for a long time, or an excuse or means to deflect pain? This exercise will help you understand how intentional and conscious your speech is, so you can use the power of words to improve your life.

Figure 11-1: write down your reasons for writing what you did about yourself.

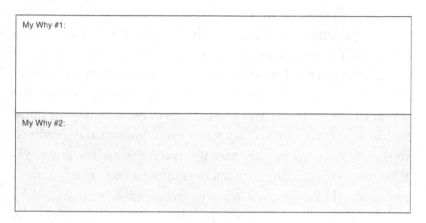

The Healing Power of Sound

The power of sound, music, and speech to heal your life is beyond profound. I'd call it a downright miracle that we all have access to. Because sound has the power to heal, it also has the power to destroy, and as such, you must use it wisely. Let's start by thinking about the last time you said something bad about yourself or someone else in jest.

People often think they say things they don't really mean or are just joking, but that is not ever true. Everything that you say has some grain of truth to it, or you would never utter those words to begin with. Dark humor is used as a way to try and heal the pain we carry, making it more bearable by normalizing it and making light of it. So why do people do this? It's because of the strong connection between emotions and words. Speech is how we unpackage and release what we're feeling, so those emotions don't stay bottled up inside. When you speak your feelings, you acknowledge them. You see them. You are giving birth and life to them, which gets them out of the mind, giving them less power over your thoughts.

By speaking something, you hold space for it and create a container for its expression; this starts the healing process of those feelings evolving and growing into something beneficial. Your mind likes to focus on what was, but your speech has the power to shape the way you want things to be, both in your mind and in life. Healing can't happen when emotions stay confined to the mind, but given the space to express themselves, any negative emotions, including painful or traumatic ones, can find their resolution. Holding space for any feeling gives you the ability to love and honor it. A loving, positive energy can heal even the most painful wounds and help you find purpose in the midst of pain.

Remember earlier when we discussed mental health as a spectrum of well-being? Talking about things is a powerful tool to unburden the mind and open the heart. I recommend every person have someone they can talk to about anything and everything. Maybe that's a close friend, family member, therapist, or ministerial guide. Your sounding board is not there to solve your problems or make you feel better about them but to help you hold space for your healing journey and be fully present with everything going on inside of you.

If something as simple as your words can start to heal deeply held wounds, think about the impact positive music or even mantra can have on your life. There are many different ways to approach this. You can use music or mantra to change your mood, clear your mind, get rid of stress and anxiety, and even give you more energy. You can use them to target a particular element to enliven and energize it. People often use soundwaves and vibration in chakra and energy healing. Music can help you relax, unwind, and get better sleep. Each type of sound will have a different effect, and this has been known for thousands of years and used in cultures around the world. A systematic example of this is found in Indian classical music, as each raga is known to have a different effect on the mind and mood. Depending on how the particular blend of sounds impact the mind-body connection, listening to the right raga at the right time can have a profound impact on well-being. Think about how this might apply to your life. Do you wake up in the morning and put on the same music you'd listen to during a night out at the club? Probably not. And are the relaxing things you'd listen to first thing in the morning or before going to bed the same things you'd use to motivate you at the gym? Definitely not.

What kind of music do you listen to? I'll bet it reflects in your personality and mannerisms. If you listen to happy, uplifting music, you are apt to act this way. If you listen to angry music, you're likely more prone to getting upset about situations. So are you listening to happy music because you're a happy person, or are you a happy person because you listen to happy music? It's both. The thing to remember here is that you can use music to change how you feel at any given time and start to write a new chapter in your book. If you see something you don't like, you have a ton of tools now to start changing it. Breathing, meditation, food, exercise, and even the things you find yourself listening to. How awesome is that?

Physics states that everything in existence has its own vibrational (sound) frequency, and this includes diseases and illness. It's been theorized that if you know the frequency of a disease, you could eliminate it completely with sound. The visual illustration of this, that I'm sure you're aware of, is a wine glass shattering when an opera singer hits a high note. When the pitch of the note matches the resonant frequency of the glass, the glass shatters. While our technological capacities might not know how to find the exact frequency of any object and match it, sound has been used in mainstream medicine to bombard and break up gall and kidney stones with sound waves through a process known as lithotripsy. I'm very curious to see how we'll continue to evolve our societal understanding of vibrational frequency to heal and harmonize lives. The power is there; we merely need to expand our knowledge and understanding of it.

Affirmations & the Mind

When you speak a thought out loud and that thought has a will or intention to it, your thought becomes an affirmation. Working with affirmations is a powerful way to create your vision of life more quickly and to draw things to you when you work with them in the right way. World-renowned author Susan Shumsky, whom we heard from earlier, has a lot of good things to say about affirmations. In fact, affirmations are core to her daily practice. She says, "The important thing about affirmations is to use them consistently, on a daily basis. Audibly state your affirmation with absolute conviction and authority, pretending as though your higher self is saying it through you."

Susan mentioned three key points: speaking your intention out loud, speaking it with conviction and authority, and acting as if your higher self is the one saying the affirmation. These are three of the four key things you need for an affirmation to work. The fourth piece is to truly believe what you are saying. This ties into speaking it with conviction, but speaking with conviction and real belief in your words are different. You must believe an affirmation in order for it to work. Speaking it with conviction is what helps you to achieve results more quickly, but believing it is what makes it work in the first place. The main reason affirmations fail to work for some people is because they are saying things they don't really believe to be true or possible for them, and that can do more harm than good. Saying something and setting an intention to it that you don't really believe is possible sets you up to fail, and this will undoubtedly diminish inner prosperity and self-confidence. It can even create a negative thought form that makes you doubt anything you say, thereby diminishing the power of speech in your life.

Another important concept to understand about affirmations is the way in which you structure them. Saying, "I will not get sick," is completely different than saying, "I am completely healthy and well." The universe, God, or whatever you call the underlying consciousness in all things, hears the vibratory frequency of the words you speak, not the way in which we string words together. If you say the word "sick" the universe hears that and thinks that is what you want, even though you want the opposite. This is why you must phrase words positively, so your real intention is heard loud and clear through what you say and how you say it. If you are sick, saying, "I am healthy and well," may not be the way to go about it though, since you know that is an untruth in the present moment. Try something like, "My body is empowered to heal itself quickly, and I have everything I need to be healthy and well."

There's an old saying that if you always speak the truth, what you say will always come true. Being mindful of what you say is a great way to expect excellence in yourself because speaking truth does add power to your words when you know that what you say can be fully trusted. There is no way for the subconscious mind to sabotage your success. Here's a simple formula: If you only tell the truth 60 percent of the time, only expect 60 percent of the things you speak as affirmations to come true. If you speak truth 100 percent of the time, expect everything you say to come true.

There are many spiritual traditions and even some theories in physics that believe time is not linear. A good way of looking at an affirmation is that what you are speaking is so true that it has already come to pass. In a non-linear sense of time, this is true. You may know what you are destined for even though not all of it has yet come to pass. You contain everything that was, is, and will be inside of you; when you choose to speak something into reality is when you manifest it in tangible form, and that is what makes time linear.

Use Your Speech to Cultivate Purpose & Positivity

Here's an exercise to help you start working with affirmations and speech in a productive way that will enable you to align what you say with your beliefs and intentions. For the moment, forget everything you've learned previously about affirmations and positivity. Let's start from scratch and build an authentic dialogue with yourself.

I want you to stand in front of the mirror and say five positive things about yourself. Things that you like about yourself. Focus on how this makes you feel. Once that's done, I want you to stand in front of that same mirror and say, "My life is healthy and well." How did that statement make you feel? Did you feel the same as when you said those five good things about yourself? I bet you did not. My experience working with people has shown that even if a statement you're saying is technically true, you won't feel connected to it unless it's something that's authentic and coming from inside of you, in this moment. If you don't feel that deep inner connection, an affirmation will not work for you, because your speech is not aligning with what you're feeling.

If you want to make your words hold power so that the things you say come to pass, start by having an authentic self-dialogue each day with you and the mirror. Tell yourself at least five things that you like about yourself, then tell yourself some of the things you don't like too. Be honest with yourself. You can be honest without shame, blame, or guilt. If you find something you don't like about yourself, think about ways you can start working on it and make that statement out loud.

For example, here's something Mary wants to work on: "I don't like when I don't speak my mind when talking with friends." Mary can then take this statement and turn it into small, simple things she can do. "The next time I'm with my friends, I'll make sure to speak up about at least one topic everyone is talking about." Bam! It's that simple. Creating an authentic self-dialogue helps you to be present, mindful, and align your speech directly with feelings. This is how change begins, and this is the starting place to build personal and powerful affirmations from.

Instead of using an affirmation to help you reach a goal, begin using these true statements about yourself as affirmations. The more you say these true things and recognize how they make you feel when you say them, you'll learn when the things you say aren't connecting in the same emotional way and you can analyze why. Continue to build on your dialogue and move it in the direction you want to go. Instead of saying, "I am happy and well," take stock in how you feel right now and the things you are specifically happy about and the things in your life that are going well. By focusing your affirmation away from broad, blanket statements to something personal to you, you can make the power of words work well for you.

Your challenge is to take five to ten minutes each day to have a dialogue with yourself. Get to know how your words make you feel. Identify that very individual feeling you get when your words 100 percent align with your thoughts and emotions, and keep moving all of your speech in that direction. After a month of this, you'll have a clear picture of how to start creating personal, positive affirmations that really connect with you and work for you. You'll also notice a huge difference in how you relate to yourself and others. It's only possible to have clear and authentic communication with others when you are able to have clear and authentic communication with yourself.

The more positivity you can include in your speech in a completely authentic way, the quicker you'll get to where you want to be, which brings me to my last point on speech and aligning it with your intentions. When you're dealing with an issue or obstacle, never possess it. It's not yours. Don't use words like "my" or "mine." I hear so many people saying "my cancer" or "my fibro," and it gives me shudders every time I hear it. That disease does not belong to you, unless you want to keep it forever. Refer to disease or obstacles as "it" or "the." Saying "the cancer" is very different from saying "my cancer." Disconnect the personal association from anything you don't want to be a part of your life. I never, not for a single moment, owned having fibromyalgia. I kept it at a distance, recognizing that it was not a part of me, just something that was cohabitating with me temporarily. That made it possible for me to heal. Everything, including life, is only temporary, so don't let these temporary difficulties get you down. Use the power of music and your speech to uplift yourself and others, and watch how things start to shift for the better.

CHAPTER 12

CREATE YOUR SACRED SPACE

Creating sacred space is important to any healing journey and journey towards purpose. Remember earlier how I described creating space like you're creating a container? This becomes quite literal and real in this chapter. Sacred space, per its name, means filling your space with sacred energy. This can be your home, your office, or even just your room, depending on your living situation. It's a way to make your space your own and to ensure your space contains the energy you personally need to succeed. Perhaps even more importantly, it keeps energy out of your space that would be harmful or detrimental to your life.

Because knowing yourself and what you need is a process that takes time, I've put this as the last chapter in this section. Trying to figure out what you need at the beginning would be solely a mental exercise and a waste of time because knowing yourself comes down to experience, not a mental concept. When you create a reality based on a mental construct that lacks experiential wisdom, that construct will collapse under the weight of your accumulated experiences as you grow. Then it will feel like you're constantly rebuilding instead of being on a steady growth trajectory towards success, which is not good for emotional well-being. We need to feel full and fulfilled in order to feel constant stability in life. Creating sacred space at the right time will help with this. There are two sides to the coin of creating sacred space. You'll first need to learn how to clear and protect your space energetically, then learn how to fill that space with the energy of whatever brings you into a state of harmony.

Cleansing & Protecting Your Space

Every thought and emotion will leave an imprint not just on the people who experience it but also on the space where it occurred. This means that, both consciously and subconsciously, you'll be affected by the places you spend time. Sometimes the effects are so subtle that you don't notice them, whereas in others, the effects will be pronounced. You probably have places you love to spend time. Have you ever thought about why? Maybe that corner coffee shop has an upbeat energy and is a good place for you to feel energized and get work done, so you go there for that reason. Mentally, you might assume this would be the case with any coffee shop, but experientially you know that's not true. You'll love some places and not connect with others, and it all comes down to the vibe in the space.

Since thoughts and emotions will leave their imprint on places, learning to clear these imprints in your home can help maintain peace of mind and harmony in your life. Life is messy and relationships are complicated. You'll have times where you get angry, sad, and feel hurt by something. Then you'll have times where you feel joyful, loved, and full of energy. The goal of creating sacred space is to fill your home with as much positive energy as you can so that it can help sustain well-being. Just like we use meditation to clear out space in the mind by digesting our thoughts and experiences, we can use tangible techniques to clear our physical space and neutralize any energy that has depleted the positive energy you've cultivated.

One of my favorite ways to clear out energy is to smudge with a combination of cedar, white sage, and sweetgrass. White sage purifies, cedar offers protective energy, and sweetgrass brings in an energy of joy. You can add a bit of lavender to this if you want to evoke peace and relaxation. The act of smudging combines the physical activity of the ritual itself with your clear intention of cleansing your space, and it works. I use smudging anytime there's been strong feelings of anger or sadness because I don't want those energies hanging out and impacting my future decisions. I also use it as general maintenance every couple of weeks, just to open up the space and make it feel more expansive.

Talk to any real estate agent if you want to see how energy in a space impacts people. If someone is looking to buy a place, and five places are essentially equal in terms of price and desired amenities, the deciding factor comes down to how a home makes you feel. I've worked with real estate agents to energetically clean properties that weren't selling to turn them around and have them sell quickly, even with people who don't believe in energy work. The results speak for themselves.

Once you've cleansed your space, you'll want to put up boundaries to keep out anything unwanted and build a container to hold the energy you want to impart. When you don't have a container, any energy you put into your space will dissipate quickly. By creating a protective container, the energy you cultivate will stay in your space longer. Here's a quick exercise for that:

1. Sit in the middle of the largest room in your house and visualize a protective, colored energy coming out of your root chakra area and starting to coat your entire home—walls, floor, ceiling, and windows, rather like paint. Paint is a good

analogy because paint bonds to the wall and doesn't go away.

2. For the windows, focus your intention that your energy is not a permanent barrier but a permeable one that allows energy to go out, but does not allow negativity to come in. The walls, floor, and ceiling should all be a permanent barrier.

3. The color that you visualize may change from day to day as you do this technique and you can use color to help understand the energy that makes you feel the most comfortable and secure.

4. Repeat this exercise every day for a minimum of seven days, doing the visualization for whatever length of time is needed to coat everything in your space in your protective energy.

5. After the initial seven days, make sure to repeat this exercise at least once a week to maintain the integrity and strength of the boundaries you've created.

6. If you ever leave your space (maybe you move to a new home), make sure you do the reverse exercise of tearing down the barrier and either dissolving it into nothing or reabsorbing it back into yourself so that you aren't leaving your energy behind in what will soon be someone else's space.

Make sure to use your energy and not what you would consider purely God or divine energy, as it won't have the same protective effect. You are a physical conduit of divinity, so using your own energy already imparts divinity into your space. When you get into a regular routine of cleansing and protecting your space, you'll notice a tangible difference in how you feel; you'll be more centered, harmonious, and ready for what life brings your way.

You can use things like saltwater sprays, crystals, and aromatherapy as a way to cleanse and impart the energy you want to create once the container is in place. No matter what technique you use to build positive energy, combine it with your clear intention for best results.

Architecture & Interior Design for Well-being

Let's now take the concept of sacred space to the next level. You can build a home from the ground up and decorate it in a way that imparts mind-body wellness. LEED certified buildings led the way with green and environmentally sound building materials. The WELL Building Institute has taken wellness in architecture design a step further to incorporate human well-being into their standards, implementing requirements like use of natural light and air and water filtration. Ancient traditions like Vaastu Shastra and Feng Shui further bring balance by incorporating sacred geometry and the energy of the directions and elements into design, décor, and colors to facilitate the highest level of mind-body well-being.

Each direction contains its own energy, as does every color and element. When building a home with mind-body well-being in mind, the layout and décor of the home is a focal point. For example, you wouldn't want to put a home office in the part of the home associated with cooking or the fire element: fire is destructive and transformative, not one for building creative energy. Likewise, you'd want your bedroom to be in a place that facilitates relaxation and sleep and to decorate it accordingly, which is an entirely different energy than you'd want in your living room or a kid's playroom.

Building commercial and residential spaces to facilitate well-being is something I've become passionate about because where you spend time has a huge impact on your mood, mindset, and how you feel about yourself. By working directly with developers and architects, I feel society can make a paradigm shift that automatically supports sustainable well-being for everyone. Speaking of sustainability, building homes and offices to facilitate well-being and more diversity is one of the UN's Sustainable Development Goals. It's globally recognized that we need to do a much better job of building in a way that supports well-being and not just profit.

If you can find a home built to wellness standards, I highly recommend getting it. It'll be worth your investment. If not, there are simple ways you can quickly facilitate better energy in any home through its layout and décor. Do you have a home office or desk where you work from? Make sure when you're sitting at the desk you are facing north, east, or northeast. This will provide sustained energy and productivity without getting drowsy or mentally sluggish compared to a south or west facing desk. If you can change your desk space at work, opt for the same thing. If you are a creative type, face east, as the extra energy imparted by the eastern direction can evoke creativity.

Sleep is essential for everyone's health and well-being, and the direction your head is pointed when you sleep can make all the difference. Have your head pointed south with your feet pointed north when you lay down. This aligns your body with the earth's electromagnetic field and makes for better, more sound sleep. Feng Shui and Vaastu believe that having your head pointed west can contribute to bad dreams, and north is never acceptable. East is fine, but you may find you have very active and vivid dreams, as the east direction brings energy. Try for south, southeast, or east when arranging your bedroom, and you'll notice a difference.

The use of color in a space will amplify the natural energy it contains and directly affect your mood and energy levels. For example, in a bedroom, it's best to have calming and soothing colors that promote rest and good sleep, and in a living room you want colors that promote harmony and happiness. A child's playroom should be filled with creative, loving energy. Here's a table showing how colors can affect your emotions.

Figure 12-1: colors & their impact on mood and emotions.

Color	Mood & Emotions Elicited	Where to Use
Black	Power, exacting, unformed feelings.	Small accent pieces.
Red	Excitement, anger, passion, love.	Small accent pieces, artwork.
Peach	Creativity, warmth, security, optimism, nurturing.	Wall color, artwork, décor. Creative room, children's playroom, or bedroom.
Yellow/Gold	Positivity, prosperity, courage, glamour, energy.	Artwork, décor, accent wall color.
Green	New growth, renewal, life force, success, healing, abundance, refreshing.	Wall color (pastel or mint shades), accent wall, kitchen, décor, and artwork.
Blue	Cooling, calming, trusting, spiritual, healing, good for sleep.	Wall color in bedrooms or bathroom, furniture, artwork, décor.
Purple/Violet	Connected, imaginative, majestic, ambitious, dignified, holistic viewpoint.	Accent piece, accent wall, artwork, décor.
Lavender	Gentle, soothing, relaxing, inspirational.	Wall color in bedroom or bathroom, home furnishings, artwork.

If the layout and décor of your home doesn't align with universal principles, this can cause problems with mental and emotional well-being, which as we've seen has a direct connection to physical health. As you now know, there are universal principles at play regarding use of colors, elemental forces, directions, and their energies; you can use these principles in the design and décor of your home to help harmonize your own individual constitution.

For example, if you are a fire element person, using cooler tones for paint and décor will help you stay balanced and focused. Too many warm or hot colors could provoke frustration, irritability, or agitation, especially in places like bedrooms, which are supposed to facilitate rest and sleep. Hot, fiery colors can also spark anger in some people, which is not good for any family dynamic.

Too much of anything in life will lead to imbalances, and this is especially true when working with your own constitution. Like tends to seek out like when, in fact, we need a counterbalance to feel our best. A way to use vibrant warming colors like red, gold, or yellow for people who are already fiery types is to use them as accent pieces: a chair, stool, piece of artwork, or even a small accent wall in a room. This way, you appease the natural desire to use things that are like yourself, while not overdoing it and causing mental or emotional disturbances. You can also tone things down by using lighter shades of paint, like a very mild pale yellow or peach, which tend to brighten up a space without the overstimulation more vibrant shades can evoke. Depending on the specific personality, you may opt for more neutral shades or cooler tones altogether. Finding the right balance is important when creating your own sacred space.

People who run on the cooler spectrum of energy, or those who have more water and earth elements, may find those mild, warming colors pleasant and uplifting, whereas a sharp, vibrant accent piece may be all that's needed to perk up a space. Since the water element is strongly connected with life force, think about having plants in your space—living greenery that needs water to flourish or the use of biophilic design. The kitchen is a great focal point for water element people and a space where you may put in the extra effort in decorating or renovating to make the biggest difference in mind-body well-being.

The beauty of creating sacred space is that when you understand basic principles of space and how your space affects your temperament, you can create the space that works for you. Here are some things to consider: use the questions below to start determining how to use your space to benefit well-being in your life.

Once you have a clear idea of where you spend the most time, what your current challenges are, and the way that you relate to color and décor, you can start setting a personalized plan for how to improve your space. Maybe it's as simple as getting a couple of nice accent chairs in your living room or repainting the walls in your bedroom to facilitate a better night's sleep. If you work from home, ensuring the space allows you to focus and maintain energy levels is important. Experiment and create something that works for you.

Cluttered Space, Cluttered Mind

You now have some effective strategies for creating and maintaining your space, both in terms of energy and aligning layout and décor to suit your needs. Any strategy you work with can reap tremendous benefits, but how successful any of them will be comes down to how well you eliminate clutter in your space. A cluttered space is a direct reflection of a cluttered mind.

1. What colors help you feel relaxed?
2. Are you attracted to mild or vibrant shades?
3. When you focus on a vibrant shade for two minutes, what effect does it have on you?
4. Do you prefer a minimalist aesthetic, or do you like to decorate?
5. Will you use art to decorate your walls or leave them blank?
6. What is your favorite room in the house and why?
7. What direction do you like to face when chilling out?
8. Does your space have a lot of natural light?
9. What rooms in your house get the most use?
10. Do you ever work out of your home?

One powerful life hack for creating mindfulness is to clean and organize your home. Creating sacred space in a home is a mindful way of recognizing that your home is a container of your energy and that your personal energy works together with the energy of your space to create a purpose-driven, healthy life. Keeping your home clean and clutter-free will have a direct impact on keeping your mind focused and clear. If you find your home is slipping into the clutter zone, you can use this as a tool to recognize when your mind needs some extra TLC. Take a moment to reflect on your mindfulness practice and whether you're taking time to honor it. If not, get back to it, and that clutter may just resolve itself or, conversely, clean up the clutter first, and it can help you get back into a regular mindfulness practice. I find it nearly impossible to meditate in a cluttered space, so you may find yourself cleaning first to get back on track instead of the other way around.

I use a game when it comes to cleaning my home. I start in one room and clean it first and, when necessary, move things temporarily into other rooms so as to get the first room cleaned quickly. The thing is, in this game, once a room is clean you can't move junk back into it once you get to the next room. This forces you to find a permanent home for all of your stuff, while allowing you time and space to focus first on the rooms that get the most use and prioritize them in your busy schedule.

If you have places in your home that are permanent zones of clutter, this is likely due to compartmentalized areas in your mind that need some extra attention. If you have areas of your home that are nearly always kept clean and clutter-free, look at what the energy of the rooms represent, as that can reflect your mind is much more expansive and clear in these areas.

Look at question six that you answered above. What is your favorite room in your home? Make sure to keep this room clean and clutter-free at all times, even if it's not the seemingly most important room to focus on. The fact that it brings you joy means that keeping it in order can help keep you feeling upbeat and positive about life. Happy decluttering!

PART III
THE SETBACKS, SOLUTIONS & VICTORIES

Now that you've completed the first two parts of this book, take a moment to fill in your entire WELL Method blueprint. This is your personalized plan for cultivating and maintaining purpose, health, and overall well-being. You've picked things for your plan that are important to you, and they represent your goals, talents, and inner inclinations. Every roadmap starts with a goal, and from your goals, a plan is formed. Once your WELL Method plan is complete, it forms a clear picture of what you need to do each day in order to reach your goals and create the healthy, purpose-driven life you want.

What I love about The WELL Method is that it takes things that are seemingly unrelated to your goals and uses them as the fuel to accomplish everything you want to accomplish. Therein is one of the big secrets of life: universal principles hold true in all situations, and you can use them to make every facet of your life successful, meaningful, and fulfilling. By honoring your innate talents, gifts, and strengths, as well as everything that comes from your elemental type any unique constitution, you honor yourself and God. This brings success in all things you strive for. Success is not about what you believe, it's about what you do.

Spirituality was never meant to be esoteric or unrelatable. It's something we are meant to live and experience in a profound way, each and every day, through living a fulfilling and meaningful life. Your personal WELL Method blueprint will give you everything you need for confidence, inner prosperity, clarity, and mental, emotional, and physical well-being. These are the building blocks of good decisions accomplishing your goals, making The WELL Method practical spirituality for day-to-day life. Now that you know exactly what it will take for you to succeed and get healthy, it's time to look at the obstacles that can and will arise to test your determination to reach your goals. Look at obstacles not as a roadblock but as a test of your ingenuity. They're merely there to help you shine more brightly and realize what you are capable of achieving. Highly successful people still have problems, in fact, they may have even more. The only difference is their ability to navigate through problems with ease. So don't shun difficulty—when you experience challenges, know that God is helping you prepare for bigger and better versions of what makes you happy.

You may not recognize obstacles for the opportunities they are. This next section breaks down the psychological and emotional hurdles most every person experiences on their journey, so you won't be deceived or thrown off-track. Remember, it's not the obstacle that stops you: it's being deceived and not recognizing the obstacle for what it is that stops you. Eliminate this deception and you eliminate the problem.

If you haven't yet, finish your personalized WELL Method blueprint, then dive into Part III. Let's get started!

CHAPTER 13

THE SETBACKS & THEIR SOLUTIONS

You're ready to get started with your WELL Method blueprint, so now is the time to discuss the most common obstacles people encounter on their journey and learn how to deal with them. Remember what I said about obstacles not being your enemy? Once you learn why the obstacle is there, you'll see what you need to do to overcome it. I don't want you to think about obstacles as the enemy. We become afraid of enemies or believe that an enemy is evil, and that is not the case here at all with any obstacles that come your way. They are not enemies or evil, but perceiving them as such is a normal part of growth. It's when we misinterpret their meaning that things go off-track.

Be very careful about what you label an enemy in life because anything you build up a wall to will be much more difficult to reach and overcome. The quickest and easiest way to overcome an obstacle is to make peace with it, realize why it is there, and do something differently. There's no need to attach emotions or negativity to an obstacle when you recognize it for what it is. You can even have gratitude and compassion for the experience because it's taught you more about what it means to be human and to be both perfect and imperfect at the same time.

The obstacles you experience may not seem related to your journey at all, and that's why it's important to recognize them early *before* you get off-track. An obstacle may cause a minor setback, and that's fine. Life is a process of two steps forward and one back. Getting off course only happens when you don't recognize the problem and it causes you to deviate from your plan for an extended period of time. In this chapter, we'll identify the most common obstacles and why they arise, so you'll know how to avoid setbacks and overcome any challenges that come your way. If you do find yourself off-track, this chapter will help you find your way back in the most seamless way possible.

Obstacles & Their Solutions

Obstacle #1: Lack of Consistency. Undoubtedly, the most common obstacle you'll face is that little (or maybe large and screaming) voice in your head that tells you to skip something in your WELL Method plan. Consistency is crucial for success in anything but especially in changing how your mind works and what neurons in your brain wire and fire together. If you've decided to take some time each day just for you but then you hear that voice inside saying, "There's not enough time today," or "You could get so much more done if you just skip this today," or, "This really isn't important," rest assured it's not true. It's just the mind trying to maintain status quo and do what it's used to doing.

When you feel the urge to not be consistent or to take a day or two off of something, it's because the new thing you're doing is causing pressure in the mind so that new neural connections can be built and new habits can be created. None of this comes without effort and some resistance! Building a new habit means destroying an old one, and that takes time. Stick with it and don't let your mind fool you. Being consistent each day with your new action will help solidify it in the mind more quickly. On average, it takes about six weeks of doing something each day just to break an old habit, so give your new routine the time it needs to work. Even if it makes you agitated and a bit uncomfortable, know this is all completely normal.

Obstacle #2: Negative Emotions About Your Plan. You've taken time to create your personalized WELL Method plan, and when creating it, you probably felt empowered and on top of the world. Well, feelings come and go, and you'll undoubtedly go back and question what you wrote instead of just trusting in the process and realizing that staying on top of the world all the time is impossible. When your mind tells you to not be consistent, those thoughts are accompanied by feelings. Whenever feelings get involved, it creates thought forms, and those have to be dissolved before you can really move forward.

The emotions here aren't the problem; they are normal because (1) the mind does not want to change, and (2) moods fluctuate and never stay static. Whenever you start to adopt new habits and create new routines, it's completely normal to feel awkward, off balance, out of sorts, and even negative at times, solely because you're doing something new. We tend to think of these feelings as being warning signs that we've gone off-path but, in fact, they are just signals that your mind is growing and changing, and that is a good thing! It's exactly what you want and need to happen. Happiness and stable emotions are created through consistency, so just by altering your normal routine, you'll also cause a perturbation in your mood. Instead of giving those feelings any credence, know they are normal and that if you stick with your routine, it will become your new normal and will be what makes you feel good.

You can help stabilize your mood by evoking happy feelings while you are taking part in your new routine. Stick with the new routine for a while, and those happy feelings will develop naturally. It takes nearly six months for the mind to get acclimated to a new routine and to feel like it's now your new normal. Until your mood starts to adapt, do other things to elevate your mood, like focusing on diet and neurotransmitter production. Be patient and give your mind what it needs to help you grow. Take some extra time each day and do something nice for yourself, something that makes you feel good. This will help you adapt to and stabilize your new routine quicker.

Obstacle #3: Blowing Up Your Plans. When I say blowing up your plans, I don't mean literally. I mean it as an analogy for what happens when you let your emotions get the better of you and things explode into a fiery mess of nothingness. You wouldn't be human if you didn't self-sabotage from time to time, so remember that. I'm not saying it's a good thing, but it is a very normal thing, because change can be scary. I've probably said this a hundred times already, but the mind doesn't like to change. It will do all sorts of crazy things to keep you from forming new habits.

Emotions are powerful agents of change that can create or undo things, and anger is a very powerful destructive force. The act of getting angry at your plans so that you can obliterate them doesn't mean the plan is bad, it just means you're having a hard time adjusting to doing things a new way, and that's both okay and normal. Try to not look at your new plan as an all or nothing proposition. You can't change everything at once, so pick one of your goals and commit to being consistent with it. Once you've got that under control and feel good about the change, add in another one of your goals until you feel good about it, then keep going. If you try and do everything at once, that is a recipe for failure. Small steps and consistency move mountains over time.

Sometimes, it's hard to know why you blow plans up. Take a moment to reflect on what you feel the next time this happens. What are you feeling beneath the anger? Is it fear or defensiveness? Next, remember that just because things didn't go according to plan today doesn't mean you can't change them for later today or tomorrow. Getting off-track gives you the opportunity to get back on it. No matter what you said or did, you can change it immediately and move towards your goal.

Obstacle #4: Declining Motivation or Willpower. Staying motivated is akin to a magic secret recipe. If you don't have the right support, the right fuel, and a burning desire, keeping motivation up on anything can be a challenge. Feelings fluctuate from day to day and that is normal, so just because you aren't as motivated today as you were yesterday doesn't mean anything is wrong. It means you're normal and that cultivating strong inner prosperity is important for you.

Stick with your plan, even when you don't feel like it. Motivation will return the more you are able to be consistent, even when it's difficult to be. The root of motivation is in feeling good about your plan and knowing it will be successful. The best way to show yourself your new plan is working is to focus on things that elevate your mood and make you feel good about yourself. This cultivates inner prosperity and acts as fuel for everything else, so don't underestimate the power of positive feelings. Low motivation is a sign that you're becoming depleted and need time to recharge.

Now I'd like you to look at each possible obstacle we've discussed and write down a few ideas that you feel will work for you to combat each of them. You know your elemental type, the foods that can boost mood, and the types of physical activities and hobbies you enjoy, so brainstorm how to use all of these when you need to get past an obstacle. This exercise will help you hone in quickly on what works for you. Write your personalized solutions to each obstacle below.

Obstacle #1: Lack of Consistency:

1.

2.

3.

Obstacle #2: Negative Emotions About Your Plan:

1.

2.

3.

Obstacle #3: Blowing Up Your Plans:

1.

2.

3.

Obstacle #4: Declining Motivation or Willpower:

1.

2.

3.

Responding to situations is a conscious choice. Here are three things that enable me to respond to life and not react to it:

1.

2.

3.

How to Get Back on Track

You now know how to recognize the real problems that come your way, and you've likely been able to use the solutions above to nip some of the obstacles in the bud. But what happens when you can't nip it in the bud and you've found yourself off-track from your goals and plans? Not to worry, this happens to everyone. Don't fool yourself into thinking that other people are perfect with their plans and you are the only one who's had a setback. That's just negative self-talk the mind likes to spew to keep you set in your old ways. The truth is, everyone will have a *big* setback at one point or another. I have not met a single person in all my years of teaching, having friends, or dealing with family where anyone perfectly navigated everything. Welcome to the side of being human that no one wants to talk about.

Recognizing that you are off course or are in a slump is pretty simple. If you're not honoring your WELL Method plan and the goals you've set for yourself, you are off course. If you committed to doing something in the plan, then changed your mind about it or completely forgot to do it, you are off course. If you've been making up rationalizations and justifications about why your plan is stupid or why you haven't been following it, you are off course. Remember, rationalization and justification are your two biggest enemies on the path towards purpose and success.

Get Started. The first thing to do is start. It's that simple. Use your personal WELL Method blueprint as a way to get back on track. Odds are, if you're off-track, you're not following the plan you've created for yourself. Start with what you've written under expect excellence, as these are the day-to-day habits that'll help build inner prosperity and create new habits. Make sure there is something on your list to do each day that makes you feel good and builds inner prosperity. This is where to start. One of the things I do is start my day with a cup of tea. This habit brings comfort and joy and is a reminder that consistent things are meant to be joyful not tedious.

Use Your Elemental Strengths. The next thing to do is to look at what went off-track and identify why. If you can identify the emotion or thought that triggered things, you can use that emotion's elemental counterpart as a way to get back on track. For example, if it was anger and blowing up plans, look at everything you've learned about how to mitigate anger and the fire element through food, décor, mindfulness, and more. If it was due to fear, you have an equally powerful set of tools that we've discussed. If it's because the changes made you feel off-balance or sad, work with the water element, and do things consistently that promote positive, flowing energy and happiness.

Use your innate talents and elemental strengths to set things right. Do what you are good at and what makes you happy. Cultivate your elemental talents. Just by working with your talents, you start to bring things back into harmony. Life gets off-track when you don't fully utilize what you've been given because it stagnates energy. Keep building inner prosperity, keep your energy flowing and open, and implementing your WELL Method plan will become easy.

Build Inner Prosperity. Getting back on track requires a healthy dose of inner prosperity, so whatever helps you cultivate it, focus on that. Sticking to any type of plan is hard, and the reasons that we don't stick to plans often has nothing to do with the plans themselves. It has to do with unresolved emotional pain, lack of confidence, or some form of not feeling your best. I'm not going to tell you to heal your inner wounds because that is on God's time, not mine or yours. If it were that simple to do, no one would have problems! What I will say is that by cultivating inner prosperity, you decrease the power any emotional wounds have over you, which will help them to be healed faster or, at the very least, not wreck your plans.

Well-being in Daily Life

It's all too common for the mind to create a false projection of what it means to be well and whole. This is because the mind likes to see things in terms of endpoints and what we've accomplished, but cultivating well-being is a daily exercise with no endpoint. What does well-being really look like on a day-to-day basis?

Let's start by looking at what well-being is not. Your WELL Method blueprint is a path to follow, not a destination to reach. Following it perfectly won't get you to your goals any more quickly than following it imperfectly. Perfection is not the goal we're looking for; the sign of success is that you keep picking yourself up each and every time you fall or go off course and come back to creating healthy habits for yourself. Perfection is an illusion. Strive for happiness instead.

If you look at well-being as a process, not a destination, it's about small steps taken daily. The easiest way to accomplish this is to stay consistent with your plans, do something each day that cultivates inner prosperity, and follow the steps in chapters 6–12. The more you are able to synergize mind, body, and soul harmony, the better you'll feel each and every day. Well-being for some people may look more like a destination than a process, and that's okay too. It may mean getting off all medications and healing the body from disease. It may mean not getting sick anymore because you've learned how to take care of yourself and what works for you. It may mean having personal time each day to focus on your health, goals, or dreams. If this is you and you have a specific goal in mind, make sure to carve out tangible milestones to these goals that indicate you're moving towards them.

In my opinion, well-being comes down to the small things you do every day that make you feel great about yourself. My morning cup of tea and going for daily walks are some of the things I do to promote well-being in day-to-day life. Anything that enables you to follow the four cornerstones of The WELL Method is a reflection of well-being in daily life.

CHAPTER 14

THE VICTORIES: LIVING A PURPOSE-DRIVEN, HEALTHY LIFE

Everyone is born with a profound reason for living, and it's up to each of us to learn what that reason is. Life is a puzzle to be solved; learning what you are good at and why you are here is one of the most fulfilling parts of life, both for you and for others. Your purpose is given to you not just to make your life a happy one but as a way for you to help others. Serving others is what brings meaning to purpose and brings the deepest satisfaction in life.

Meaning & Impact of Purpose

It's a fundamental universal principle that we are not islands, and nothing in this world is self-sufficient. Everything in existence is here to make something else flourish. We all need help to be successful, healthy, and fulfilled. For example, rain nurtures plants; then those plants provide food to humans, insects, and animals. Humans, insects, and animals help nature survive. The cycle goes on and on, with the purpose of each part of nature never being there to fulfill or sustain itself. Humans are the same. Our purpose is not for us but for helping others thrive.

It's easy to recognize how creating the life you want is fulfilling, but there is a larger puzzle you fit into. Whenever you are successful and happy, you enable other people to be successful and happy too. You give people the hope and inspiration they need to cultivate inner prosperity and deepen faith in themselves. Much of this communication is subconscious, but it's something people feel even if you never speak a word directly about it. Being successful also gives you the ability to guide and mentor others along their journey so they gain the skills they need, and it helps you have compassion for the struggles everyone has or will face. When you see the big picture, making sure that you succeed and fulfill your purpose is really not about you; it's about elevating others and making a positive impact on the people in your life. Purpose creates synergy to all of our experiences, making even the simplest things meaningful and profound. The measure of a person is not in what they have accomplished themselves but in what they have enabled others to accomplish.

Living a meaningful life means living an impactful life. How is your purpose helping others in need? I've found that when people doubt their purpose, the primary reason is because they have yet to figure out how their purpose will impact the lives of others. Doubting can be a good thing because it means you are questioning; just don't let that doubt derail you in the process of figuring it all out. Doubt itself can be brought into question, and that's a powerful way of keeping inner prosperity strong.

Purpose Creates the Path

Instead of needing to have the answers to everything all at once, or even knowing how you'll impact others, let the path itself teach you as you grow and follow your purpose. Once you know what your goals are and what you are striving for, the path will become clear. You need both your starting point and an end point in order for God to create a path. Without the endpoint or goal, God and the universe at large can't steer the ship because you're not letting them know what you want. It's impossible to create a line connecting two points if you don't have the endpoint. Remember that a goal can always be changed later, or, once you reach it, you can set a new one, but you have to have a start and endpoint in order for your personal trajectory to create itself. The more details you have about what you want to accomplish along the way, the more markers your path will have to show you where you're at on your journey.

For example, as a writer, I get to decide how I want to use that skill to fulfill my purpose. How much of an impact do I want my books to make? Do I just want to be a writer, or do I want to be a New York Times best-selling author? Do I want to earn money from writing, or do I want to make a career and living out of it? What purpose do I want to accomplish from writing? How many people's lives do I want to impact? These are the sorts of questions I've asked myself to help shape my path. What questions can you ask yourself about your own purpose that will help your path to create itself? We get to dream of what we want, and then God takes all the information we provide and weaves together the web of life and experience in a way that enables us to reach these goals, so as to be happy and fulfilled. You create the goals and God creates the path from your goals, so be clear about what you want.

Using The WELL Method to Reach Your Goals

There is only one limiting factor you have in reaching your goals: yourself. If you want something badly enough, the means will be brought to you to get it. The WELL Method was created to optimize every step on your journey so that you get the best possible results out of everything you think and do. The more you expect excellence in yourself, live your purpose, and come from a place of love while maintaining the harmony you need in life, the more you can up-level what you're able to accomplish and the impact you'll make. It's a spectrum of energy, or vibrational frequency, that I call destiny vs. fate. When you fully support yourself and enable yourself to succeed, you can reach your destiny. When you don't enable yourself to succeed, you'll succumb to fate and get less success and joy than you were meant to have. Here's the thing: destiny is created through willpower and personal effort, whereas fate is created by everything but you. It's chance. If you have the power to get what you want out of life, why would you ever leave your existence up to chance?

If you live by WELL Method principles, it's impossible to succumb to fate. The WELL Method works because of mind-body-soul synergy, where one plus one can add up to five and not two. Synergy is key to success because there are only twenty-four hours in a day and only so much personal effort we can put in. Synergy takes care of what we can't do on our own and ensures we're on a path towards a profound destiny and not lost in the weeds of fate. Everything that you do to empower and enable purpose in yourself sets a stronger foundation to build upon. The stronger your foundation, the higher you can rise.

The mind-body-soul synergy you create through The WELL Method creates inner prosperity and fuels your purpose, and it also makes each of these pieces stronger individually. Here's an example: By meditating, you create a healthy mind, body, and emotional state. You deepen your connection with God. And you enable yourself to be responsive to life instead of reactive. One action has affected five different outcomes. This is a tangible example of how synergy works, and it's the same with anything you give your energy to, not just meditation. Success is impossible without synergy, so be mindful about what you give energy to. Make sure you pick things that will impact multiple areas of life and keep building on itself, just like we discussed in chapters 5–12.

Wellness & Purpose in Day-to-Day Life

Because overall well-being is something we are always cultivating, you may underestimate what it looks like in day-to-day life. It's not the big things we do that make the most difference but the small things that keep mind, body, and soul synergy strong. Living your purpose means being ready when opportunities arise and also learning to see opportunity in every situation that comes your way. Some days, maybe that's cleaning your bathroom. Others, maybe it's diffusing a tense situation at work or with a spouse. Maybe you get a promotion at work or the big break you've been looking for. My definition of well-being means being ready for whatever life brings you and learning to keep inner prosperity strong in all situations.

Granted, cleaning your bathroom is not nearly as exciting as getting a promotion at work, but you can learn how to respect it for what it is—an opportunity for consistency and better energy in your home. It also helps promote mental well-being since outer cleanliness leads to a calmer, less cluttered, and less anxious mind. All of those are a win-win for overall well-being, and the simple act of cleaning your toilet helped you get there. Pretty profound, isn't it? I bet you're just aching to get up and go clean now! If not, you might try this instead.

Remember what we discussed earlier about doing something each day consistently that makes you feel happy? This is the most important thing you can do to promote both well-being and purpose. The mind craves consistency, so by making a daily routine that makes you happy, you are forming neural connections that make your happiness a priority. It's far too easy with all the hustle and bustle to get bogged down worrying about others and not making time for yourself. While those may be good intentions, you do much more to help others by setting a good example for yourself. Communication is 70 percent or more subconscious, so your example speaks louder than words ever will.

Simply put, make yourself just as important as everyone else you are trying to help. By doing this you will be more successful in helping yourself and others than by neglecting what you need for overall well-being. We discussed this and some other useful tips in chapter 4. Revisit this and see how these tips can help you cultivate well-being in day-to-day life.

How Does Purpose Create Success?

Here is the million-dollar (or more) question. Does living your purpose and living a life focused on mind-body-soul well-being really create success in career and relationships? Yes, yes it does, and it all comes down to charisma. Charisma is born from the synergy and positive energy you're creating. It's a magnetic energy that draws people and opportunities to you. Charismatic people all have clarity of their purpose, confidence in themselves and their actions, and the courage to go after the things they want in life. The WELL Method helps you create all of these in your life, and they add up to a powerful recipe of success. Charisma affects how people relate to you, how much they trust you, and how much confidence they have in you. When you emit clarity, confidence, and courage, people feel it and will have more faith in your abilities. This means that you are apt to get the things in life that you work for and put your energy into, in career and personal relationships.

Charisma creates a palpable energy field around you, but don't misunderstand it as being likeable. Charisma is different. It's a magnetic energy that goes beyond like and dislike; even if someone dislikes you, they can still feel drawn to you and the positive energy you emit. This gives you the advantage and manipulates results in your favor, throwing chance out the window. All things else being equal, you stand a higher chance of success in all matters than people who lack charisma and aren't living their purpose. This is not something you can fake; it's something that happens authentically when you genuinely feel good about your life.

Inner prosperity leads to outer prosperity, which can be translated as money, wealth, power, or successfully reaching your goals. You may not have all four, but you'll end up with the ones you truly want in life. Material prosperity can be fickle. If a person lacks inner prosperity and they come into wealth, it can be difficult to hold on to it. The person who first creates a foundation of inner prosperity then accumulates material wealth and success is better prepared to keep it long-term. Don't ever underestimate the power of synergy in mind, body, and soul working together as one. It gives the ability to stay healthy, weather all storms, overcome any obstacle in your path, and accumulate as much success as you can dream of. The question then becomes, how large can you dream?

CHAPTER 15

KEEP MOVING FORWARD (OR CONCLUSION)

This book wouldn't be complete without discussing how to keep moving forward and how to redefine your purpose when things change in life. Something can fully be your purpose here and now and then not be your purpose twenty years from now. We discussed this briefly earlier, but I'd like to go into more detail because purpose is an evolving concept, as is consciousness, so let's look at purpose as it relates to consciousness itself.

It's no easy feat to define consciousness, but let's look at it as the combination of your connection to the whole cosmos, including God, your awareness, and your experience of life. It's everything wrapped into one. How you relate to any and all of these will impact your perception and understanding of life. The deeper your spiritual connection becomes, the more you'll try to impact the world in a positive way. The more experiences you accumulate in life, the wiser you become. Spirituality, awareness, and experience all impact each other, just as the mind, body, and soul triad impact each other. As you grow and evolve your understanding of life, your personal fulfillment, and your experience of life, it's only natural that your sense of purpose will also shift.

At its core, purpose will always be connected to how we choose to help other people, animals, or the planet. It's service to the greater good. What changes in our sense of purpose is how we choose to impact the world, and why.

Stage in Life & Impact

At different stages in life, it's normal for people to want different things. A younger person is going to have the need to accumulate experience and wisdom and to define who they are in the world. For someone in their twenties or thirties, having a career that aligns with one's ethos on life is more important than to someone in their sixties or seventies who has retired and no longer has the same driving factors governing their life. Of course, money is also a driving factor in how people choose to live their purpose. If you have to work for a living, your career and lifestyle choices will likely be a lot different than if you don't.

I've found that people often try to hone in on what their purpose is without taking these things into consideration, but that's not possible. Since purpose is meant to fulfill you, it can't be an abstract or intangible concept. It has to be connected to what your day-to-day life looks like and what is possible for you here and now. We also have the habit as humans of relating purpose to a particular goal or set of goals. Cultivating a meaningful and healthy life is relative, not absolute. Once you take a step toward your goals, you then take another step and another. Eventually, you'll find that you've accomplished your goals. Then what? Does that mean your purpose is fulfilled? If you're still alive, you still have a purpose, and it's time to redefine what it means relative to your current experience of life.

As your consciousness continues to grow, as you reach your goals and succeed in endeavors you set out to accomplish, your sense of purpose must also grow and evolve. For some people, this means expanding the scope of impact while keeping the same focus on the work itself. Instead of working to impact 1,000 people, perhaps you set a goal to positively impact 100,000 people. Expanding the scope of impact can also mean redefining your "how" or the method of fulfilling your purpose. Some things don't scale without change, which gives you the opportunity to try things in a new way.

Fulfilling All of You

Another thing that commonly happens as people expand consciousness and grow is that their main focus in life shifts. It can be troubling to feel that you've worked towards one purpose then are shifting it completely to something else. I want you to take a moment to see this from a new perspective. Remember that purpose is never an absolute thing and that your expression of it will grow and change. In addition, if you feel the need to shift course, that means something deep inside of you is seeking expression in a way it wasn't previously able to, and that's a wonderful thing. It's a clear indicator that you've grown and evolved as a person—so much so, that for the whole you to be fulfilled, it's time to focus on a different piece of that whole.

There are different reasons why this happens. Most often it's because we heal broken pieces of ourselves, and this part no longer needs the attention it once did, allowing us to focus on other parts of our being. It's also common for highly evolved souls (which is likely you if you're reading this book) to be really good at doing multiple things. Once you feel you've mastered one thing or become an expert in it, it's very normal to want to use your time to continue evolving another way to express yourself. I believe this stems from an inner recognition that there are so many ways you can use your talents to fulfill your purpose that we feel a deep desire to be at our best, in all possible ways. God has given each of us so many talents and only so many hours in each day.

I view cultivating your talents as a profound and practical way to worship God because you're honoring and using what you've been created with as a way to fulfill yourself and make the world better. Whenever you honor your talents and seek self-improvement, you're directly communicating with God and your highest self. Being conscious of this helps to deepen your spiritual connection and find fulfillment even in the smallest of things.

Try New Things

You know by now how important consistency is. It's equally as important to recognize when consistency has turned into stagnation of your creativity. Perhaps you haven't noticed much change, and it feels like life's passing you by; not that anything is wrong, but could it be better? Trying something new is a great way to find out. Changing things up is a great way to get out of a rut if you're feeling stagnant, and it's the only way to increase the impact of your work or make a change in its scope. Anytime you change up your routine and do things differently, you'll evoke new emotions and uncover pieces of yourself you may not have known were there. This can give you new ideas that contribute to your sense of purpose and help cultivate meaning in a new way. Trying new things is also a guarantee that you are constantly evolving and growing in consciousness. There's a dance that happens between consistency and shaking things up, and your accumulated wisdom is what shows you the right time and place to make a needed change. If you are fully serious about expecting excellence in yourself, trying new things should be your motto. Never be afraid to do something differently, because every experience will teach you something and help you better define who you are and what you want out of life. New experiences also make it easier to adapt and feel meaning when you're in the process of redefining your purpose. If you're not used to making change, you'll not feel good even when change is exactly what you need.

Most rules that we create are meant to be broken at one time or another. They are there to help us reach a goal, but it's very important to ensure following the rules doesn't become the goal itself. As a part of trying new things, challenge your own rules from time to time and see how this helps you grow as a person. Does it better inform your decisions? Does it show you that you were already on the right track? Does it make you feel grateful for what you have? You'll be surprised just how much shaking things up and trying new things can impact your perspective on life.

Keep Moving Forward

Lastly, but most importantly, no one is perfect. We all have goals, plans, purpose, and desires, and we will all have setbacks from time to time. When things change, when you're figuring out a new purpose, setbacks are even more common until you solidify a new routine. Just keep moving forward. What you did even one minute ago doesn't have to impact you for another minute if you get up and do something different. Remember that goals are there to help you accomplish your purpose, but they are not a destination to reach in and of themselves. If you miss a day of meditation, sit and be silent for two minutes, then get back on your schedule. If you miss your exercise routine, do a minute of plank pose. Did you just find yourself yelling at your spouse or kids? Take a moment to breathe. You can always do something small that shows just how capable you are of setting things right, at any time, in any situation. This will help you navigate through change.

The human mind likes to think it's all or nothing to reach your destination, and that is a lie. Small acts make just as big of an impact in the mind as large ones do. Keeping your mental and emotional health strong is your priority for cultivating inner prosperity. Remember that mental health and mental well-being are a spectrum not an absolute. If you miss your workout, doing a minute of plank pose won't give you the same motivation that your normal routine does, but it will get rid of that nagging voice in your head that tells you you're a failure. Every time you pick yourself up and keep moving forward into the unknown, you're making mental health a priority by ensuring you don't fall into what I call mental sickness (which is different from mental illness). When you're sick with a cold, you get better quickly because it's only temporary. It's the same with mental sickness; it's a temporary state of being unwell that you can fix quickly through effort and self-care.

Every year or so, or during a major life transition, make sure you reevaluate your WELL Method blueprint and see if anything needs to change to help support your new goals. Nothing stays the same forever, and there is beauty in that. You get to experience more of what life has to offer and become more fulfilled in the process. Change is the only constant in life, so embrace it with open arms, knowing you have everything you need to find fulfilment, live your purpose, and cultivate meaning every step of the way.

ACKNOWLEDGMENTS

I'd like to thank everyone who has made this book possible including the entire Post Hill Press team, my mentors, teachers, and the people who have inspired me to pursue my dreams. A special thanks to my literary agent, Lisa Hagan, for making this happen, to Debra Englander for believing in me and my book and being a phenomenal editor, and to my awesome graphics designer, Hayden Brown. My deepest gratitude goes to everyone who has contributed their knowledge and wisdom to this book including my friends and colleagues Dr. David Friedman, Dr. Teitelbaum, Dr. Susan Shumsky, and Dr. Josh Axe. You're all amazing and I am grateful to know you!

ABOUT THE AUTHOR

Jaya Jaya Myra is a bestselling author, TEDx speaker, TV personality, and mind-body wellness expert teaching the connections between spirituality, purpose, and health. Myra created The WELL Method to teach people the four cornerstones necessary to create a healthy mindset and holistic approach to life.